# IMAGINAL FIGURES IN EVERYDAY LIFE

## Stories from the World between Matter and Mind

Mary H. Harrell, Ph.D.
With a Foreword by Robert Romanyshyn

Chiron Publications/
innerQuest Books
a division of Chiron Publications
Asheville, NC 28803

To
my son, James Michael Jr.
the imaginal angel to whose memory I dedicate my writer's life

To
my daughter, Lauren Elizabeth Fortgang
luminous child

To
my husband, Stephen Edward Sapos
Wisdom Keeper

Published by Chiron Publications/ innerQuest Books/a division of Chiron Publications
Asheville, NC 28803

**www.ChironPublicatons.com**    Also visit: www.innerquestbooks.com, www.AshevilleJungCenter.org, & www.maryharrellphd.com

Cover Design by Cornelia Georgiana Murariu,
Cover art by Cynthia Clabough Ph.D., Oswego, NY 13126
Part of the artist's "Temple Series". The cover temple belongs to the goddess, Anna Perenna.    Author Photo by Shannon Hellinger

Grateful acknowledgement is made to the respective publisher and author for permission to reprint the following previously published material:

Excerpt from Rainer Maria Rilke: Duino Elegies, David Young (Translation, with Introduction and Commentary), 1978, reissued in a Norton paperback 1992. Published by W. W. Norton & Company. This translation was originally published in FIELD, Contemporary Poetry and Poetics, issues 5 through 9, Copyright 1978 by W. W. Norton & Company, Inc. Reissued in a Norton paperback edition 1992. Rilke, Rainer Maria, 1875-1926. Translated by David Young,

Excerpts from Judy Grahn's The Queen of Swords, 1987, from the poem titled, "Descent to the Butch of the Realm." Reprinted by permission of Judy Grahn to whom rights to the work have reverted.

Printed primarily in the United States of America.

ISBN 978-1-63051-354-2 paperback
ISBN 978-1-63051-355-9 hardcover
ISBN 978-1-63051-356-6 electronic

Library of Congress Cataloging-in-Publication Data

Names: Harrell, Mary H., 1948- author.
Title: Imaginal figures in everyday life : stories from the world between matter and mind / Mary H. Harrell, Ph.D. ; with a foreword by Robert Romanyshyn.
Description: Asheville, NC : Chiron Publications/innerOuest Books, [2016] | Includes bibliographical references and index.
Identifiers: LCCN 2016011817 (print) | LCCN 2016019809 (ebook) | ISBN 9781630513542 (pbk. : alk. paper) | ISBN 9781630513559 (hardcover : alk. paper) | ISBN 9781630513566 (E-book)
Subjects: LCSH: Imagination. | Fantasy. | Visions.
Classification: LCC BF408 .H3145 2016 (print) | LCC BF408 (ebook) | DDC 153.3--dc23
LC record available at https://lccn.loc.gov/2016011817

In soft whispers and quiet evocations
We are called by soul to seek the depth of a thing,
To wonder what else, or who else is present
In the cavernous mystery of lived experience.

- Mary H. Harrell

# FOREWORD

*Imaginal Figures in Everyday Life: Stories from the World Between Matter and Mind* is an extraordinary book. On the margins of the ordinary its extraordinary quality makes the book a much needed corrective to the ways of seeing and speaking about psychological life in the discipline of psychology.

Dr. Harrell's exquisite prose offers a kind of psychological writing that is rare because it marries content and style. What she says is expressed in how she says it. Her language is an invitation to enter into those experiences that are presented in her stories, allowing the reader to know them from within rather than only to know about them from a distance. This kind of writing is responsive to those depths of soul which psychology ignores, disregards, disbelieves, dismisses and marginalizes. In its STEM initiative it would mandate that psychology model its language on science, technology, engineering and mathematics. While such a style of discourse does correctly address the quantifiable dimensions of human experience and behavior, in its exclusion of the humanities it tends toward becoming an ideology.

In her exquisite prose Dr. Harrell recovers from the margins those epiphanies of soul exiled in psychology, those qualitative dimensions of experience that make us most human. In this regard her book is a therapy of culture.

But I would be remiss if I did not say at the outset that reading Dr. Harrell's book is also a personal therapeutic experience. As a reader I was re-minded of those subtle moments in life when, as she demonstrates in her stories, the extraordinary erupts from the ordinary and shines, like fireflies in the night, with a glowing luminosity. Carefully distinguishing at the outset between memoir and autobiography, her stories are responsive to the appeals of soul making its entrance through the material world. Over and over again one begins to see the splendor of the simple, the miracle of the mundane, the luminosity of the numinous as well as the shadows of experience that accompany one's descent into the underworld, the landscape of soul that depth psychology has called the unconscious. Dr. Harrell is a witness to these evanescent epiphanies that are neither matters of mind nor material events. She is a witness whose stories point a way through which the reader can accompany her as a companion. Reading her stories I am reminded of the poet John Keats who invited us 'to call the world the vale of soul making.' In that place between matter and mind, in that place between worlds, on that thin line between fact and fiction, dream and reason, idea and image, one needs a poetic sensibility. Dr. Harrell has such a sensibility and alongside her we learn to make that call.

Each of the tales that Dr. Harrell presents opens a specific dimension of the subtle world of imaginal realities. In the first story, 'Coffee Hour,' we get a glimpse of the numinous depths of the simple daily event of taking one's coffee in one's garden. 'Unbidden Angel' is a meditative and moving description of the grieving process and the healing capacities of the imaginal world. 'The Raptor' describes an encounter with a bird of prey, which parts the thin veil between the human and the divine world and allows the glory of the divine to manifest itself in the guise of a wounded hawk. 'I am Inanna' is a beautiful depiction of the power and presence of the Feminine Archetype, and in 'A Nation Dreams its Violence' and 'Crones in the Shadowlands' Dr. Harrell insightfully demonstrates how one navigates in these landscapes of soul. In this context her book has practical applications. It is a primer for practicing psychotherapy between worlds, and in addition her book suggests ways of researching the transformative effects of imaginal experiences.

The Irish poet Brendan Kennelly describes the difficulty of bringing language to visionary experiences. The problem, he notes, is the afterwords afterwards. Dr. Harrell has found a way to bring words to her experiences of the imaginal world. Her book is not just a theoretical defense of the reality of the imaginal world between matter and mind, though it is scholarly and well grounded. Her book is a living experience of that world whose words are the cloth of wonder and not its shroud. Indeed, her book, which is a joy to read, is an example of what a psychology of wonder can be.

In the final pages of her book Mary returns to the garden where she began and in that place she offers the reader a final gift. Imagine working in the place between worlds as learning how to tend the garden! Imagine the psychologist between worlds as a gardener!

Robert Romanyshyn, Ph.D.

Emeritus Professor of Psychology at Pacifica Graduate Institute and an Affiliate Member of The Inter-Regional Society of Jungian Analysts. The author of seven books including *The Wounded Researcher: Research with Soul in Mind*, Dr. Romanyshyn has recently published *Leaning toward the Poet: Eavesdropping on the Poetry of Everyday Life*.

# ACKNOWLEDGMENTS

This book would never have been published without the wise and careful tending by the Chiron Publications family to whom I owe so much. I am deeply indebted to Editor-in-Chief, Dr. Len Cruz who read my manuscript and acknowledged it as a worthy story of healing and transformation. His walking with me from the first reading to publication date has been a grace to me, and a gift. Chiron's Publisher Dr. Steven Buser, whose gentle encouragement and faithful responding to an ongoing stream of queries has become a steadfast partner in the work. To count on him for timely direction as the work gently wound itself from initial manuscript to living dialogue has been a blessing to me. Emily Scott-Cruz enriched the work with her keen editorial eye, so often preventing me from embarrassing myself with unnecessary grammar and mechanical blunders.

Of the most able team at Stan Info Solutions, I am amazed at the power of their commitment to this project. I wish to thank and bless them for their patience, and their immense skill at copy-editing, typesetting and organizing. Because their team members, under the astute leadership of Rani Xavier, deeply understand how to produce a book, the style and organization of every page underscores the depth of its content.

I gratefully acknowledge Jeffrey Raff whose profound Jungian perspective has guided me to the final pages of this volume. He has often gone with me to the world between matter and mind as a familiar traveler providing illumination so that I did not get lost. He has been an unflinching mentor and a companion on my own path of soul tending, a path so mightily reflected in each chapter of this book. The kindness and integrity with which Veronica Goodchild remembered my aims in the earlier versions of *Imaginal Figures* when I could not, are precious gifts to me. I am indebted to Robert Romanyshyn for suggesting 18 years ago that my work could be of value and that my writing had merit. I am grateful too because he is a tender and brilliant teacher who taught me well and changed the way I know the world. Robert's lifetime commitment to the development of a poetic sensibility toward the world has certainly birthed that same desire in my own writer's life.

I affectionately acknowledge the seven members of my writing group: Jean Ann, Barbara Beyerbach, Bonita Hampton, Sharon Kane, Tania Ramalho, Roberta Schnorr, and Chris Walsh. They are fellow scholars whose many questions have brought clarity to the work, allowing me to bring analytical psychology beyond the clinical setting. The brilliant work of graphic design artist Cynthia Clabough brings a dimension of the imaginal to my work that only visual narrative can. I am grateful beyond words that she chose to give her art a home on the cover of this book.

One cannot investigate inner life, much less survive its painful onslaughts, without a strong ego and a good bit of insight. I am deeply indebted to the generous wisdom and counsel of Dr. Nagy and Dr. Teague both of whom guided me through significant life transitions. Of them I can say that they are trustworthy men of great intelligence and integrity. And from both of them I received the gift of healing.

The first story for this book was written more than two decades ago but, it would never have developed into its potential without my finding a sacred womb at Pacifica Graduate Institute, in Carpinteria, California in the fall of 1997. It was there that I learned to speak the language of soul, and there that I found a perfect blending of compassion and academic rigor. To my most amazing teachers there, and my worthy classmates, I offer my great gratitude by writing this personal and scholarly contribution to soul in the world. It was in their good care that I learned to trust the language of the heart.

I offer heartfelt acknowledgment to my siblings JoAnn Stoudt, David Stemrich, Michelle Stanton, Joseph Stemrich, Marella Gregory, and James John Stemrich (who visits me often in the imaginal realm). All six have shared my life journey and love me well. To my two children Lauren Elizabeth and James Michael, who lay claim to my deepest heart's longing, I extend humble gratitude and boundless love. I extend my unending respect and gratitude to Lauren's biological father Jim Fortgang who, like a loyal centaur, remained deeply connected to our daughter through a 3,000 mile distance, encouraging her, appreciating her gifts, and always putting her needs above his own. Without his unfailing love our daughter's light in the world might not burn so bright.

To the many imaginal beings who visited my dreams and imaginings until I surrendered to their wish that I write, for them and for me, this public narrative of a woman's inner life. I acknowledge that they and I are connected through the whispers of love. It has always been my intention that I do justice to our journey together.

Dearest husband Stephen, you are the man whose generous heart enlivens my days and illuminates my nights. To you I extend gratitude from my deepest being for all the passages of this manuscript that you have read, and for the many days and nights you have smiled upon my writer's journey.

# ABOUT THE ARTIST

Cynthia Clabough lives in Oswego, New York, where she teaches graphic design and illustration at the State University of New York at Oswego.

## ARTIST STATEMENT

My creative process is similar to cooking a full-bodied pot of stew. In a base of early "good daughter" training rhetoric and pop culture musicals are chunks of new age explanatory literature and feminist manifestos; spiced with quasi–intellectual, academic references. You could say I believe, literally in "stewing" about things.

Since early childhood I have tried to comprehend the world around me by working it all out visually by creating allegorical narratives as a way of sorting things out. The work offers me the opportunity to frame an investigation, to bathe in my imagination as a way of gaining clarity. Through this process of creating, I begin to understand.

The work seen on the cover was created as part of a series of "Temples" in which I imagined a previous civilization where women were at the center of the theological world. This particular temple belongs to the goddess, Anna Perenna, and honors the power of women to rebuild and transform themselves from shattered to whole on their perennial quest to live through each year. The work is also about my mother, Anna, who taught me that endings become beginnings.

# AUTHOR'S COMMENTS ON THE COVER ART

The cover image for this book, like each story I tell within the following pages, possesses a particular totality. That is to say, it needs no reason for being, beyond itself. Visual artist Cynthia Clabough has given you and me a creative gift in which, vivid colors, gorgeous composition and, an allegorical narrative gather, like a perfect poem, in the artist's space.

And still, I wish to share with you why Cynthia's visual art resonates so vibrantly with the intention of this book, an intention best described as an invitation to live life more imaginatively. In doing so, one begins to live consciously in a dimension whose language is love, and whose path is transformation through suffering.

I respond to Cynthia's composition exactly as I might respond to a dream, allowing the rich symbolism to speak to me, and thereby to become enlivened as a communication from soul. Image in art, as image in a dreamscape, wants to be deeply experienced, both with one's eyes and with the organ of the heart, an idea that many in the field of analytical psychology refer to as the imaginative capacity.

Cynthia's images, like the experiences within this book, take me to an enchanted world, a world in which imagination is vibrant, real and deeply informative. In her rendering, women stand in the temple as modern goddesses. For Cynthia, these women lived in some long ago civilization. Because imagination is keen to break all rules of time and space, it is not surprising that for me, these goddesses are symbolic of an evolving feminine consciousness in the present, a development at the personal, cultural and ecological levels of experience. To me their gestural tone speaks of transformation, and also, an easy ownership of their divine status. These goddesses have transcended a patriarchal order, and seem to bask in the light of the moon, symbol of the archetypal feminine.

You will notice that in the space between the moon and the temple (the soulful and the divine) there is great animation, and delightful starbursts fill the sky. One sees a breaking through of a royal light over the horizon. This sky portion of the "dream art" underscores for me the idea of illumination, seeing that which otherwise remains in the shadows of awareness. In this nod to the practice of shining a light in the darkness of the unconscious, we see a reflection of my author's commitment to look deeply. The journey toward feminine consciousness requires one to navigate dark spaces of being, and on rare occasions to experience those evanescent moments in which a transformative note sounds bright and beautiful in the darkness.

Cynthia's visual narrative also speaks to me of a divine order that is grounded in the earth, just as her temple goddess figures are grounded. This image offers great hope that the emergent archetypal feminine will neither be lost to hubris, nor environmental disregard. This emerging feminine consciousness, instead of holding false dominion over the earth and her creatures will live with them in deep respect and harmony. One can imagine in this artistic story, a consciousness in which, connection with the environment and kindness between orders neither bows to a modern scientific method, nor a patriarchal theology.

Notice too, the stag in the lower right. He is the unconscious archetypal masculine, unconscious because, though he drinks from the earth and her waters, he is not yet aware of the quality of inter-being that he and the earth (the feminine) enjoy. The relationship between the stag and the water (another archetypal feminine symbol) is one of unconscious mutuality.

And finally, when through art or dream, we encounter symbology in which land and water meet, we are likely transitioning from one dimension of consciousness to another. We are poised at a border crossing if you will. As each story in the following pages becomes an investigation of different dimensions of the imaginal, what you will see as a constant theme is the idea of transition: transition through the realm between matter and mind, between unconscious and conscious and between dream and waking states. When Cynthia's art found its new home on the cover of my book, it was for me a synchronistic moment in which, an "other" chose to direct both artist and author to collaborate, at the borders of our craft, for the sake of soul in the world.

# Contents

# INTRODUCTION

It is my intention that, as I explore the intriguing world of imagination and the figures that dwell therein, three goals will be met. First, that my stories will contribute to an expanded conversation about the imaginal domain, an area of study still in its infancy. Second, because I enter this realm through personal accounts, I aim to speak in a public forum of my own lived life and perhaps more importantly, of the imaginal figures who share both my journey and the writing itself. And lastly, it is my goal that for all readers, particularly clinicians using their organs of imagination, new and deeper avenues of healing will become available.

I am often asked, "To what end do you pursue your many questions about the mundus imaginalis?" These questions include: In what ways might the imaginal realm manifest? Can one cause it to appear? Does a world as vast as the imaginal possess common threads, perhaps common intention, or a common source? How might one relate to a subtle presence? My answer is always the same, and always causes my heart to quicken, "I ask these questions for the sake of soul in the world." My ultimate aim is to provide avenues of entry to the imaginal domain for the many thoughtful readers who are not Jungians, but who wish to understand the mysteries of the unconscious within the context of their own lives.

## THE CALL OF THE JAPANESE DANCER

I open this introductory section by sharing the way in which I came to explore imagination and her images. Simply put, I had the idea to write this book almost 14 years ago, and immediately, a dream followed in which two important events occurred: (1) my unconscious soundly weighed in, encouraging me to move forward, and (2) the appearance of a figure, from outside my psyche, allowed me to intuit that she would guide me in the work.

For me, reality has always been experienced in the three realms that I address in this introduction: matter, mind, and the in-between, neither/ nor realm of soul. Because my organ of imagination has long been active, the world of what society thinks of as ghosts, visions, the paranormal, the real quality of dream images, and instinct as a respected mode of being has been both familiar to me and an important aspect of my psycho-spiritual functioning. However, until now, I have chosen to be silent about the soul-scape through which I navigate my life.

I understood intuitively and early in my development that I live within a societal consciousness in which empirical science, reason, and the reality of mind and body exclude imaginative figures (as ontological realities) from respectable, and until recently from scientific discourse. Some scholars of modern physics refer to this type of limited societal consciousness as "the zone of middle dimension" (Capra, 1991, p. 64), a zone in which people only consider as real that which fits into a familiar and classic (Newtonian) physics model, rather than the broader construct of subatomic or cosmic models of reality. To consider imaginal experiences as real seems too far a cognitive stretch for so many.

As an example of the exclusion of the imaginal, a friend approached me, several years ago, with a tale of a personal experience. It had been necessary for him to travel into what was, for him (because of certain negative affects and beliefs), a hostile and frightening valley in Pennsylvania. Though he feared entering the valley, he tried to force himself to proceed, because going through this area was the most reasonable route to his destination. When he approached the valley, he was so frightened that he couldn't move forward, ending up, staying in a hotel for two days unable to get out of the bed, almost paralyzed. During those days, he was so incapacitated by fear that he could not even call his wife to say what had happened, leaving her frantic at his two-day disappearance.

The best he could do in the end was get into his truck and take a circuitous route to his destination, costing him almost one extra day of travel, but avoiding the valley. However, when he saw me four days later, he was smiling and excited as he reported what happened when he attempted to go through the valley on the homeward leg of the journey, "As I entered my descent into the valley, I knew without seeing that a loyal wolf was above me, sitting sentry on the roof of the truck. I could feel a protective light surrounding the wolf, the truck and me. I knew, that we could descend, move through, and leave the valley without harm." He was amazed that forces within another realm had helped him in this unusual way.

Without missing a beat, after recounting this soulful lived phenomenon, he pronounced, "But I don't believe it," and happily walked away! With that one sentence, he chose to deny his own experience in order to quickly reenter a model of reality in which he found comfort, one in which all things are logical and reasonable. He never spoke of the encounter again, as if there had been neither the light, nor wolf. Notably, my own acknowledgment of the reality of imaginal figures within these pages plays out quite differently.

In keeping with their interactive and purposeful spirit, the figures within my own imaginal sphere began constellating and commenting early in the writing of this book. On the night I slept after writing the original ideas from which this work has flowed, I had a dream. The dream, years later, remains vivid and numinous (the Greek for "divine nod"), no doubt, because the figures within wished to comment on the work at hand. In the following passages, I will share the dream and also my understanding of its meaning. Some may wonder how I knew what I knew. The answer is the same for any dream interpretation—as one wonders about the meaning of the dream, one feels a resonance within, often a loud inner voice that says, "Yes!"

And so my dream begins:

> I get out of a car and approach a home in the country. On the porch to greet me are many members of my family. I notice as I climb a path toward them, that an old garden encircles the home; years of neglect and overgrowth do not obscure the great design and beauty that claims it still. Its paths, weaving here and there, and its variegated shades of greens and multi-textured shrubberies, speak of a marvelous structure that under-girds the garden. What I witness, speaks too, of a gifted and loving gardener.
>
> As the group (curiously lacking in animation) observes my approach, I see what they do not, that to my left and their right, dances a young girl, dressed in Japanese classical garments. What is most striking is that the numinous quality of the girl's movements— her grace, her blending of music, form, body, soul and spirit—are

not of this world. In the dream, I struggle to find some way to organize the otherworldly experience. I am frustrated because I try to experience it with my senses and knowledge of the world and find those capacities inadequate. My frustration is nothing though, in light of the wonder and beauty of her dance. (Dream Journal, 1999, p. 53)

## WHAT DID THE DREAM FIGURES WANT?

I have been moved by classical Japanese dance, wherein reality was of a worldly beauty. Not so, the dance and the dancer of this dream. I knew as I watched, that her dance transcended that which my material senses perceived. In the dream, it was the bodily gestures within the dance that deepened the experience of the mundus imaginalis; the gesture linking affect and image brought a sense of awe. As I witnessed her dance, I remember knowing that I was in the presence of a figure unlike any other I had encountered before.

As I have mentioned above, this girl was on the right of my family, who did not notice her. I wondered if my dream family held the symbology of a larger social order, one that did not hold her in consciousness. The thought crossed my mind that perhaps this social order could not see her in the dream, because it was not open to the realm in which she dwelt, a truth expressed in the inability of so many to hold in awareness figures from the mundus imaginalis. As I considered this possibility, my initial observation of this family's "lack of animation" popped into awareness, bringing a new "aha," that is that anima is the Greek for soul. Without soulful participation, they could not experience this being who was anima personified. On the other hand, I could, at least within the dream, experience her, feel the otherworldly marvel of her dance, her soulful aliveness, her elegant innocence, and her unmolested beauty.

In the dream and afterwards, as I thought about its meaning, my sense of profound gratitude and wild excitement signaled that she represented more than an aspect of my own interiority. This dancer seemed to be a figure, a guide, from outside of my own psyche. I awoke knowing that such a dance could not come from me alone, as my mind and body are bounded by the limitations of my own human nature. She, with her extraordinary presence, was a figure more fantastic than a human figure could be.

This girl also possessed a quality of otherness, suggesting that she had an autonomy all her own and that her presence in my dream was what Raff (2000) describes as psychoidal. The ambiguity inherent in some imaginal figures allows them to be, at times, both inner figures and also representations of outer figures (meaning, in this conversation, outside of my own psyche). In a private conversation with Raff (June 2001), he described a related, though often overlooked, phenomenon that one can experience an image of a psychoidal figure who is not the figure itself, but represents the actual form of the figure, just as in a dream one can experience an image of one's father without being in the actual presence of the father. In my dream, I experienced both her image and her being. I would describe my encounter with this imaginal figure as deep and uniquely intense. The depth refers to a quality of soul that lies closer to one's center than one usually experiences. To have shared a space with her has resulted in a felt sense that my life can be organized into two parts: before and after encountering her. In the language of soul, she brought a sense of peaceful certainty that a fate lying deep within shall be realized.

I knew, too, that an internal impulse or life force that I will call "ghosts" brought the dream and also lived within it. They too would guide the work, asking of me embodiment and a joining with them in expression. Experiencing them, with the exception of the dancer, to be representations of my manifest self (my own psychic center), I could trust their guidance.

That the structural undergirding of the garden is still visible, though somewhat muted, conveys a sense of feminine relatedness in the imaginal. By this I mean there was the promise that imaginal figures would work with each other and me, for the sake of the study at hand. The garden also suggests birthing and groundedness. I wondered if the birthing and grounding would relate to the central challenge of this book, to re-imagine that world, and at least some of her figures, which, until now, lay dormant, and in dusky neglect, intricately woven within a matrix of possibility.

Finally, this dream held a cosmic quality, a suggestion that the consciousness of a larger culture, perhaps another realm, is near, but needs others, who are more open, to help welcome and tend that other reality, neglected in our post Cartesian world. This modern domain overvalues science and reason much like a weightlifter who has become so muscled and bulked that he has lost his capacity for fluid and flexible functioning. It felt as if postmodern society itself is ready to step into a new paradigm in which, in the imaginal sense, ghosts and angels are seen as vibrant relational creatures, part of our own personal and cultural complexes, and inhabitants of a forgotten realm.

I awoke with a profound knowledge that ghosts who dwell in my own softer, quieter, elusive realm—grandmother, mother, son, and also cultural ghosts—brought forth the dream, and the deep meaning within. I heard their voices, not in words but in the language of heart and image, whispering "Well done," a nod perhaps to having begun this work: to bring forth in memory, voice, and texture this large relational community.

The workings of memoir would tell tales and dreams of my own lived life and the lives of my angels; more importantly, it would attempt to bring conscious joining to the two worlds in which I experience life, one animated by matter and mind, the other by image, and perhaps open the enchanted field between the two. A profound peace enveloped me, and does still. I knew that the dream and all of its images could be trusted. I would be supported in the work by the self and also by a transcendent divine. Together, we would continue the work of the loving gardener in the dream, tending that which dwells in the rich soil of the imaginal.

## IMAGINAL FIGURES

As a first definition of the imaginal realm, I'll borrow from Iranologist and scholar Henry Corbin (1997) who said that the imaginal realm is a subtle world, which exists in a field between matter and mind. Additionally, psychiatrist Carl Jung and archetypal psychologist James Hillman, as well as other trailblazer scholars, have made significant contributions to this emerging field of imaginal psychology, allowing me to draw from their work. In the pages that follow, I offer some examples of how the imaginal world (also known as the mundus imaginalis) manifests in daily life, and the part it can play in psycho-spiritual development and healing.

Central to any conversation about the imaginal realm are the figures that dwell in that large and mysterious region, not a literal world with defined geographic coordinates, but a place better described as a dynamic and real place of experience, a locus inhabited by multivocal, multivalent beings. I refer to these beings throughout this book as interior figures, images, unbidden angels, or subtle bodies, meaning figures that are neither fully matter nor fully spirit. Jung (1961/1989) spoke of imaginal figures as both personifications of internal (and often unconscious) dynamics and also as autonomous realities, as for instance in his descriptions of his guide, Philemon (p. 183). Jungian analyst Jeffrey Raff (2000) takes Jung's thought further by introducing the notion of psychoidal figures that exist outside of one's psyche. In my exploration of imagination, I consider the many ways in which an image has informed my own experience, which brings me to question the different levels of reality and the many ways in which the imaginal manifests.

## MEMOIR

Through a memoir I share my deeply personal inner experience with the wish that, as my readers witness the wonder and possibility of a life lived imaginatively, they too, will set an intention to enter and explore this awe-inspiring space.

It seems that I am writing for myself and also for my ancestors. Jung (1961/1989), too, shared an experience of feeling a call to complete his ancestors' work:

> I became aware of the fateful links between me and my ancestors. I feel very strongly that I am under the influence of things or questions that were left incomplete and unanswered by my parents and grandparents and more distant ancestors. It often seems as if there were an impersonal karma within a family, which is passed on from parents to children. It has always seemed to me that I had to answer questions that fate had posed to my forefathers, and which had not yet been answered, or as if I had to complete, or perhaps continue, things which previous ages had left unfinished (p. 233).

For me, there is a need to bring my embodied being to the act of writing with the sense that others, with whom I am linked, want their stories told through my experience of them. My ancestors ask that through this book, I answer questions that are both my own and theirs. In studying imagination, I contribute to an ancestral way of knowing, which began to develop before I was born. Therefore, mine is one of many steps toward a more developed and expanded consciousness, a long process that has been moving forward since primordial times.

It is important to note that a memoir differs from an autobiography in its emphasis on those people or events that shape one's life rather than on personal development (Abrams, 1999). This memoir surely brings significant people and events forward as they are important to my own unfolding; however, there are also figures within the imaginal domain who exercise some degree of autonomy in codirecting the path of this book. I claim that the way in which my own conscious ego and the imaginal figures interact suggests particular areas in which imagination can best be investigated, particularly through dream figures, reverie, and active imagination—an act of directed wondering and listening while one is awake. Because I write for myself, my ancestors, and other imaginal figures, the structure of this work holds perhaps a more fluid quality than that of other theoretical studies. By this I mean that there are a few passages in this book in which I seem not to be so much writing about imagination, as taking my reader with me as I am propelled into the imaginal realm where figures wait, as authors and participants. This dynamic writing process is illustrated in the first story entitled, "Coffee Hour."

## GRIEF WORK

When the story within the image combines with clinical intervention, a level of healing often results. For therapists who understand the tradition of depth psychology, particularly Jungian psychology, the link between imagination, imaginal analysis, and therapeutic methodology is implicit and also profound. In the tradition of analytical psychology, there is a central idea that within the image lies the presenting complex, otherwise known as the problem. The image, therefore, provides a map of the territory within which the therapeutic work unfolds.

My perspective, which values image as both an ontological reality and a therapeutic tool, is illuminated by Hillman (1983b). He writes that nature, or physis, is transformed by the soul's image-making capacity, or poiesis. For Hillman, the kind of images, or fictions, that heal are "preposterous, unrealizable, nonliteral, from which singleness of meaning is organically banned" (p. 102). His words describe the nonrational, nonspatial, nonlocal, and multivocal quality of imaginal material that emerges in the therapeutic encounter. He refers to these images found in the soulful domain as "healing fictions," and "the psychic healing of imagination" (1983b,

p. 102). In underscoring that image is a way to psychological healing, he writes, "It seems as if the sense of fiction becomes the goal of psychotherapy and must be the way we perfect ourselves" (p. 106). For a deeper understanding of using the organ of imagination in the healing process, you may want to read Hillman's (1983b) Healing Fiction.

A final thought on the usefulness of this work in clinical practice begins with a reminder to the reader that this is a study of the reality and the epistemology (critical investigation) of imagination. However, because image and healing are inextricably linked, the benefit of this work to clinicians is limited only by the depth, or lack thereof, of the individual clinician's imaginative capacity; the same is true for any thoughtful reader. Most of the experiences chosen for this study are ones in which an image is a partner in the work of healing. In hosting an image as well as interpreting it, all of us—my reader, imaginal figures, and I—become participants in the transferential field, working the field, and also being worked by it, for the purpose of psychological healing, development, or both.

# CHAPTER ONE

# Images in Reverie

As I write each of the two stories that follow, "Coffee Hour" and "Unbidden Angel," I describe an undulating field, a space in which the imaginal realm breaks through in unmistakable particularity, much as the rise of musical color in a compelling symphony grows, sometimes softly, sometimes explosively, filling the room with a vibratory presence, unlike that of any other symphony. As with many of my stories with quiet beginnings, there exists, in each account, a moment in which a seismic shift breaks wide open an unmistakable life force within.

Notably too, there exists in all imaginal experiences, a constellation of affects and beliefs, as well as excitement by at least one archetype, accompanying and contributing to the encounter. These contributing elements allow a "mining" of the experiences, as well as a gathering of knowledge about the mundus imaginalis and her figures. Because I intend to learn what I can about the workings of the imaginal realm, I explore after each story, the ways in which my own beliefs and affects shape the experience.

In the first story entitled, "Coffee Hour," reverie, a soulful process and an important aspect of this chapter, invites experiences of deep being, wondering, longing, and movement into multivocal levels of reality. Bachelard (1960/1971) describes reverie as an encounter with soul, a descent without fall. In reverie, he writes that every man or woman finds repose in the depths. Reverie relaxes consciousness, and paradoxically evokes poetic images that require full attention. Reverie, like poetic image, claims us, and takes us where we need to be to encounter the imaginal.

This first story situates itself in a simple yet large garden space in my own backyard, and will likely carry my reader, as it did me, to an expansive, inviting soulscape, a place where I unashamedly taste the nectar of the

Mother Goddess, allowing myself to be alive to Her juicy wonders. The beauty and grace of the natural world balance so well the many rhythms of my current inner world. My life in the present, having once been ferociously worked over, as if it were a stone being polished and refined in an impersonal tumbler, is perfectly attuned to the abundance of now.

## COFFEE HOUR

Sinking into a green Adirondack chair near my Upstate New York garden, my coffee hour begins. Perhaps more accurately this is my sacred time, having returned from the gym I am pleased to be done with my duty to good health and bodily strength. Almost before the cup reaches my lips, just as a light breeze tickles the curve of my cheek, a grand exhale erupts from within, a signal that some enchantment is about to unfold, as it often does, when I agree to allow a true exchange between the natural world and myself.

As if directed by some playful imp, my attention darts to the space between the ground and the sky above where a riotous dance ensues. The trees around me—Cherry, Silver Maple, Alberta Spruce—are awash with life, singing in a fabulous frenzy. Brilliantly orchestrated, a rhythm begins, a first whisper builds with the speed of an approaching train, until the dance between the leaves and wind bursts into a loud chorus, each tree belonging to a prescient multivocal community.

With each repetition—a first whisper of a breeze, an insistent stirring, the crescendoed whoosh ending with leaves whipping through air—a vivid anticipation of life is both born and realized, not in the grand gesture of the Rocky Mountains, but in the beauty of refined dance steps, each building upon the ones before, each creating its own hunger for the next. How does this gorgeous enchantment become itself? As the dancer needs the music, so too does the leaf need the wind. As the dancer needs the troupe, so too does the leaf need a thousand sister leaves.

Yet as quickly as it begins, like a brief measure of a musical score, it ends. One, two, three, four. Done. From a first whisper, to open armed yes, the tree chorus builds, then quiets as if a breath is done, though the air is filled with pregnant anticipation. There is no doubt that the rhythmic pattern will repeat itself, proof that this morning's arpeggio will see itself through.

Being here this morning, in the role of audience extraordinaire, thoughts intrude like uninvited guests, "Who makes this moment thus? Who creates this spirited dance?" What exquisite divine allows such beauty to present herself to me a simple coffee drinker in an Adirondack chair?

An answer comes as I gaze up, almost blinded by a shock of sun bouncing behind high branches, "Simply accept this gift. Listen as the song of each rustling branch fills you. Hear an army of field grasshoppers scratching rasped legs against tiny wings, (males singing for mates), and birds, too many to count, announce from the woods beyond, that they are here too. Experience all of this even as the leaves, first low then insistent, then wildly alive, repeat their song. Hear it, feel it, see it, smell it, taste it if you can. Don't miss any of it."

As if to say, "There's much more," a cool breeze visits my sandaled toes. My breath quickens, as this is the same fast breeze that makes the trees sing. My toes open web-like allowing my embodied soul to drink herself full. Looking toward the woods, a giggle bubbles out of me, as I notice a troupe of tall grasses, pirouetting as if above the ground. Each blade glistens with its own light, individual yet moving with the others in unison, creating ocean waves of movement. Though I have heard that no two snowflakes are alike, I wonder could this also be true of each blade of grass. Could each blade be its own unique miracle? Again an answer, not from a cool breeze but a quickened wind as she kicks up multitudes of grasses, causing each to sparkle like diamonds, crying out in tiny voices,

"See for yourself. Are we not unique unto ourselves, even as we join with others?"

Astonished, I wonder, "How could I have not seen this before?"

By choosing awareness I have become a participant in an animated, sensate world. Though I sit stationary in my chair, I amazingly find myself rustling loudly through a thousand maple branches. I experience whispers of light caught in the mitts of dancing grasses, each blade an outfielder catching a ball in the curve of a gloved hand, at once surrendering to the moment of contact, and also holding the ball in the mitt's center, firm and sure.

Like each coffee hour before, this one draws to its close. As so often happens I have not been disappointed. I will take the pleasure of this morning's encounter through my day, knowing that even with my departure, the song of the wind in the trees, the grasshopper music, and the bright dance of grasses will continue (Harrell, Personal Journal, 2010).

## A SOUL CARVED INTO ITS FULLNESS

In this first account, reverie indeed claims me, placing my being—awake, aware, and fully engaged—in the arms of the Great Mother. It is reverie that circumvents an overvalued, ego-centered, modern world view; in that act of circumvention, I am fully aware that humankind is only a small part of a vast pulsating universe. Surely, my reader noticed that in the altered consciousness of reverie, the unseen is rendered visible, and the enchantment of the world erupts. The feelings of unabashed abandon, so obvious in "Coffee Hour," flow from an encounter with the vitality and consciousness of the natural world.

I place this short story at the beginning section of my book for two reasons. First, it is a gift to my reader, as many of the other explorations within this book are of a much more weighty nature, in which I ask my reader to be with me in a descent to unknown, and sometimes frightening, loci in the underworld of soul.

This more delightful, though profound beginning story is a testament to the claim I make throughout this book that suffering and descent are preparatory and transformative steps that one must take if one's soul is to be deepened. Suffering—the royal road to a life lived within a rich and deep matrix of experience—allows one, in the end, to open wide to a multitude of imaginal mysteries and breathtaking moments.

The stories that follow "Coffee Hour" are from those times of my life which for me were difficult, yet in the end, sacramental. I was often, for instance, in the darkest of situations, finding myself without enough resources of time or money to feel confident and safe, often feeling abandoned, afraid, or profoundly confused. One story titled, "Unbidden Angel," finds me, an emotionally raw 15 year old, in the wake of glacial disorientation and loneliness, following the sudden death of my mother. And yet, the mystery imbuing the imaginal experiences of those times suggests that it was in those periods of chaotic descent to an unfamiliar underworld, where I found, in large measure, my substance and mass.

The second reason I choose to begin with "Coffee Hour" is so that, as the other stories are read, my reader might remember this vibrant, light-filled capacity of a soul, made deep through suffering. I want my reader to remember the wonder and possibility of a soul carved into its fullness. It is my intention that my reader will agree that this felt abundance is a reason enough to carry on when life's journey becomes so difficult that we feel as if, instead of breathing air, we are breathing sand.

Martin Luther King once said that life is hard as steel. I completely agree that this can be so, at times, and yet, one can nonetheless choose to claim the harsh, cold, unyielding aspects of life, and seeing suffering's benefit—soul's perfection—surrender into it. By doing so, one earns the wings to gently fold, or proudly span the distance from the end of light, to its source.

## AFFECTS AND BELIEFS IN THE IMAGINAL FIELD

On this day in the garden, this visitation by the instinctual feminine, the archetypal Mother, carries the scent of gorgeous bounty, and also, the triumph of a lumbering bear finding a honey pot. And yet that true and positive affect pales in the face of what my soul signals to me on this day: the encounter marks a return home to the best of me—me before the orphaning from my mother's death, me before the loss of family patterns and partnership after divorce, and me before the death of a sweet son whose unlived life haunted me in dark corners of experience.

One is away from home, not present in one's life, when one's inner experience seems like that of a gravely wounded animal in the isolated recesses of a barn, laying low, breathing shallow, not eating, just waiting for enough strength of heart, enough intuitive clarity, to go into the world and continue another day.

The longer one is away, the sweeter the scent of home, the more one can feel the tender warmth of her mother's open arms, or in my particular situation, the open arms of the archetypal Mother. Coming home for me, and for many who experience loss and grief, is reaching the end of a long descent into the underworld experience. I have also been privileged to witness this "coming home" in some of my patients in my psychotherapy practice, when after years of individual healing they find this return to the self.

It is clear that in "Coffee Hour" I find the archetype of the Great Mother, constellated in her most positive aspect. Here, she is not enraged at environmental disregard, not bringing tornadoes, fires, drought, or mudslides. This aspect of the Great Mother does not push against society's conscious refusal to participate in eco-respect. Here, she blesses all the imaginal figures in the garden: the grasses, the leaves, the wind, and all that enters this space. Alas, she whispers blessings to me.

It is true that every member of that enchanted world is indeed a concrete presence—the lively wind, the sound of the grasshoppers, the rustling grasses. Yet each, in the belly of the archetypal Mother, becomes ensouled. She is abundance personified. She is the juice and vitality that grants the leaf its thin-veined translucence, its supple nature; and it is her generous gust of wind that sends it dancing. All of these realities, the concrete and the imaginal, entwine within the softened consciousness of reverie.

Because the Great Mother is She who gives life, and also, in her negative aspect, the ontological force of death, we are ebullient when she smiles upon us in a backyard garden. To receive her grace is to live a mystery, in which all of life is writ large, becoming the great in-breath, the moment of the "I am here." It is exactly because she can, and does, exercise her chthonic nature—all the more when societal consciousness angers her—that we embrace and enjoy her equally powerful pleasure impulse.


## UNBIDDEN ANGEL

The following story, "Unbidden Angel," is one in which I experience a figure, neither wholly spirit, nor wholly matter, who first visits at a time when I am bereft, disoriented, and, like Jung after he broke with Freud, grounded in mid-air for a period of years. The quality of consciousness inviting this experience of the imaginal is not characterized by a softening, a gentle falling into the depths as in the reverie of my first story. Rather, consciousness is lowered, as every hill and valley within soul's geography moans under the weight of unacceptable grief.

To situate the reader within my own psycho-spiritual state on the night my visitor first manifested, I wish to share an earlier related experience, a preliminary "leaking out" of the archetype of death. Several months before my mother died in 1962, with her pregnancy moving along as planned, I dreamed that she had died and that my father, my older sister JoAnn, and I were in Jastrempski's Funeral Home choosing her casket.

I woke from the dream in inconsolable grief. My mother, who was very much alive on the morning of my dream, came to my bed, held me, listened to my vivid telling of the dream, and comforted me, saying that she was fine and that all would be well.

Although the 53 years since her death have diffused many memories, like the sound of her voice and a world of tender gestures, I still can feel the real weight of her arms and chest as she embraced me that morning, and the luscious moment of contact as her head bent to mine; she didn't speak, rather she crooned reassurance, bringing forward a depth of love that only a mother can bring to her child. Her comforting response remains a visceral part of my experience, washing over me even now, like a quiet gurgling of cool water from a mountain stream.

I discovered soon enough that those earlier intimations from the depths of shared family soul had indeed correctly imaged the subtle constellating of the death archetype, so vividly portrayed in my dream. It wasn't quite 3 months later on April 20, 1962, that our mother died of complications in childbirth, less than 3 hours after my youngest sister was born. It was shortly after noon on Good Friday.

The next day I went with my father and sister to Jastrempski's Funeral Home. As we walked down the steps to a beautifully appointed basement room, I knew which casket we would choose, where it was in the room, and everything that would be done and said—each nod of the head, the feel of the white satin lining, all of it, because I had lived this event in my dream months before. I was 13 years old.

This period of time marked the beginning of years of loss, confusion, and loneliness. I remember a deep disquiet within, as I painfully noticed that the ontology of the natural world itself seemed undisturbed, as if all was as it should be.

For instance, the daily rising of the sun, bright, whole, and warm confused and disoriented me.

"How," I wondered, "could new days begin, over and over, in a world where my mother wasn't present?"

Our family was without soul. We couldn't breathe. I couldn't breathe, and yet implausibly, we breathed nonetheless, not falling dead, in some sort of required and correct grotesque rhythm that seeped a bit each day, into the pores of our family soul.

It is in this field of a world askew, no longer reasonable, that the story below unfolds. I will tell it as simply as I recall it, and then go on to share my understanding of the nature of this figure, this unbidden angel, and the space in which we encountered each other.

I was asleep at 216 S. 14th Street, in Allentown, Pennsylvania. It was 1964; my mother had been dead about 2 years. In the haze of days that followed her death, neighbors did occasional laundry; relatives stayed for several weeks, flooding us with crash courses on childcare, cleaning tips, bed-making protocol. Eventually they would be called back to their own lives, leaving us overwhelmed and feeling impotent.

Dad had remarried in July of 1963, 15 months after Mother's death. The first order of business had been to move the whole family to Allentown, where the railroad work was; Dad was an engineer. Perhaps the idea was to give everybody a fresh start, or to give the new couple a fresh start. We didn't talk about those kinds of things. Life then was about surviving, getting from one day to the next and, not collapsing under the weight of our mother's loud absence.

We were seven children, two adults, four small bedrooms, a bath and a half, and no yard. Gone were the woods where we had hideouts, where grottoes appeared for praying, and cliffs for climbing, where fallen trees magically became great steeds, performing deeds of power and swiftness. Gone were the hordes of laughing, storytelling, loving relatives, gone the old Polish ladies who loved Zaz (my mother's nick name), braided our hair, and hung kielbasa from the basement rafters to dry. Gone were the block parties, where streets were cordoned off for dancing, celebration, and bingo games—gone all that hailed home.

On the night in Allentown when the figure first came to me, I was asleep. In my room, my single bed rested against the south wall with only two feet between it and a wall to my left, where all the closets housed Catholic school uniforms and a few "regular" clothes. Next to the closets beyond the foot of the bed lay the door. JoAnn, my 17-year-old sister, slept in her double bed, about four feet to my right. I would need to get to JoAnn's bed that night. Because I would be so terribly frightened, I was almost unable to span the distance between her bed and mine.

What woke me was an odd awareness that someone was with me. I knew where she was—at the far corner, by the door and to my left. In the years that followed, no matter where I was, no matter the room or building, the figure always waited at the far corner, and to my left. In some unspoken way, our thoughts connected.

I knew she was with me before she materialized. The way in which she materialized caused me to remain isolated in the experience because over the years, I had no words to describe the manner in which she moved from a nonmaterial presence to a subtle body, a body that I could actually see. I believed then that I was in the presence of a ghost, in the sense that the broader society thinks of ghosts.

One evening many years later, I watched a Star Trek television episode and heard the words, "Beam me up, Scotty." I was stunned to see an image of the character, Dr. Spock, disengage only to re-combine in another place, I felt familiar with that process, as it was the way of my figure. Witnessing a "materializing" experience through the eyes of a film artist was a first cultural connection to my experience and an important one in giving me at least an inner voice with which to express what I had seen.

As the form of my visitor emerged, and even before, I sensed that my apparition was not evil, which was significant because in my Catholic tradition there were injunctions about communicating with any beings that were not of the rational, material world. Unfortunately, I was not able to trust that feeling of her good intention. This kind of encounter, I feared, was like those considered dangerous to one's soul. As I continued to watch my figure materialize, fear gripped me. Her movement towards embodiment, as well as her movement towards me, was so slow that it wasn't part of the world I knew. The fear was beginning to paralyze me.

She began communicating, without words, that she came on my behalf; she wished to be with me and to give me something. I could see that her embodiment was almost complete. I found myself looking into the face of a woman whose features were yet unclear; she moved toward me like a Madonna being carried on a platform in a Mexican procession. Her movement and the bend of her head and hands were life-like and fluid.

My heart was pounding. I was like a scared rabbit before it dies of fright, its little heart too small to tolerate the demands placed upon it; sweat poured out of every pore. I felt raw, physical, paralyzing panic. The way my heart was pounding was terrifying. I did not believe a heart could beat that hard and not erupt. Never before or since have I experienced this quality of terror. All I could think about was escape.

She was going to give me the box; that's why she came. She continued to approach, hand outstretched, her movements incredibly kind and slow. As I reflect on her now, it is clear that she was doing what she could to work within the matrix of my fear.

What felt like a beloved gift of wisdom came upon me at that moment. I knew that if I could simply get out of bed, get to JoAnn, my flesh and blood, living, breathing sister, the figure would leave.

I directed my head to rise, my torso, my arms, my legs and feet to move. Fully expecting them to comply as they had done innumerable times before, I felt new horror at the realization that I was absolutely paralyzed. Moments were passing; the figure was now more fully embodied; the box was moving closer and my fear-riddled frame was not responding. I pushed for movement, felt my heart working harder, sweat pouring, and nothing. Again, I demanded movement and heard a loud internal cry, "Oh, please, God, don't let this be happening to me. Help me."

I was afraid because I had never tested my own physical limitations like this, yet this fear was far outweighed by the idea of my figure actually giving me something from another world. I was a 15-year-old girl whose world, until now, at least as I consciously understood it, had been deconstructed by unresolved grief; yet it was a familiar deconstructed world.

What was happening to me flooded my whole being. Since I was not able to trust my instinct—which told me this was a kind and loving figure—I was confused about whether this visitor was good or bad, or whether she would bring sanity or madness. My mother's death left me with no wise woman to ask. It was dark, and I was alone. And more than life itself, I did not want that box. Taking it meant connection with the figure, and completion of something so full of awe that it was terrifying.

Again I put every part of my being into physical movement. I felt my toe move. That movement was like shattering the walls of a tomb. Immediately I could feel the absence of paralysis; I shot out of bed and flew towards my sister, toward her flesh and warmth, which would ground and protect me. JoAnn was my link to a level of consciousness, which would disempower my ghost. JoAnn, who never woke that night, could bring me back to the world of the "I," the material, the world whose time and space was predictable; where I could believe that only solid bodies moves through empty space.

But there was one more shock for me that night. Only moments after my feet hit the floor, I experienced confusion. Why wasn't I in JoAnn's bed by now? She was only several feet away. Something was wrong. Looking down at the floor, I saw that it, like a treadmill, was spinning below me. I ran and ran, but never moved forward. The lady was coming toward me, still.

The same wisdom that told me that this figure would leave if I went to JoAnn, told me that I should give up running and leap like a fawn from the floor to her bed. And so I did. In that moment, the lady simply was no longer there.

Although my leap into JoAnn's bed ended whatever condition allowed my angel's visit, for 22 years she returned, many times. We played cat and mouse. She, waiting for those moments when all was still, and, my conscious awareness dim, I posting sentry over my twilight time. I grew to know the feel of her presence long before she materialized, and over the years, I became adept at outwitting her. All it took was the flick of a light switch, or later in life, the feel of warmth from my husband's back, that warmth a testimony that he was wholly flesh, the opposite of her. My figure's task over the years was to deliver the box and its contents; mine, unfortunately governed by fear, was to prevent such an act. (Harrell, Personal Account, 1986)

## A WISH TO ILLUMINATE AND GUIDE

There has been no figure that has gripped me more, over the many years of my life, as this woman. She is complicated and multivalent, both in terms of her own reality and also my understanding of her. She is the spirit-end of the orphan archetype (I, the material end, the inconsolable orphan for whom the early and sudden loss of a parent is unacceptable). She too is the spirit-end of the archetype of death, an idea in which the archetype of death is so remarkable an experience that when it visits it can create a high level of excitement that spills outside the psyche of the individual; the be-reaved becomes the expression of the archetype in matter, and the figure (or angel who visits) becomes the expression in spirit.

Perhaps most noteworthy is that my figure is also an autonomous, ob-jective figure that chose to manifest out of a wish to illuminate and to guide, a response to the wounded cry of an animal-child in pain. In this dimension of her being, she is Corbin's (1997) idea-image, an objective soul figure whose purpose is light; an idea I understand as divinely inspired illumination. Paradoxically, as I have grown in maturity and have developed a grounded ego and deeper understanding of reality, she has become a simple figure, a friend who came to support, to illuminate, and to guide. Although she remains a subtle body, her simplicity lies in a change in my understanding of her; over the years, I moved beyond a modern Cartesian/scientific model of reality.

A figure such as she does not simply appear; there are conditions, which must be constellated for such a breakthrough of the sensible world, conditions such as the presence, for example, of the archetype of death or the orphan archetype, and a mixture of affect and fantasies. I shall begin by sharing the experience of my own affect in the days before her arrival, as well as my view of the world in that tender period after my mother's death. Of value also will be an exploration of the way in which my psycho-spiritual state participated in the experience of the angel's visit. I shall end with my understanding of what the box, as well as her wanting to give it to me symbolized, as well as a final sharing of my views on my own rejection of this figure—from the time she first appeared, until my 37th year, when she stopped visiting.

## STATES OF BEREAVEMENT AND LONGING

My angel came 2 years after my mother's death, during which time I experienced constant exhaustion and breakdown, not in the sense of being diagnosed as possessing a mood disorder or a psychosis, but breakdown in the sense of being too long without my mother's touch, her voice, or her presence in the world, breakdown in the sense of bearing bereavement that weighed like a mountain on my back.

My soul felt emaciated, my psychological life withered, and my spiritual beliefs called to me to accept and to trust in God's will, but my soul could not find peace, could not accept. Unconscious rage at a God who allowed such a calamity manifested in occasional outbursts in prayer: "I demand that you bring her back now," I cried out one night as I knelt beside my bed. This outburst was followed by a devastating nightmare in which my mother appeared, vampire-like, swooping down upon me like a ghastly apparition. At 15, I viewed that horror as a consequence of yelling and even raging at God. As was my custom in those days, I talked to no one about such matters.

Daily responsibilities demanded that I attend school; no one seemed to notice that the girl that I was—straight-A student, class leader, editor of the paper—had been altered, had been placed in an average track in the new school, had stopped studying, laughing, and enjoying friendships. Life became a quagmire of burdensome responsibilities. There were chores that never seemed to end, child-care responsibilities that seemed better suited to a woman of 40 than a girl of 15 (like being told by the family doctor that it was my responsibility to give my youngest sister a rectal thermometer when she had a fever, with the admonition that if I forced the instrument rather than allow the sphincter muscle to pull it, I might rupture her intestine and kill her). I experienced a world as no safer than a glass skyscraper in a tornado. Life was fragile and frightening. The cosmos was no longer dependable, and I was too depleted to care.

I walked through my days zombie-like, finding brief moments of laugher and occasional solace in prayer, daily communion, and occasional breakthroughs of brother/sister escapades, like dancing rock and roll with the refrigerator handle as my sister and I did our nightly kitchen duty. Nonetheless, so much of life bled into a numbed state of sustained pain. One evening while babysitting my brothers and sisters, I made popcorn in what would be considered the old fashioned way. The bottom of the pan was covered with hot grease; as I rocked the frying pan back and forth to cover the kernels with oil, the lid flew off, causing the hot grease to cover my arm to the elbow, causing third-degree burns. Although I do remember the pain, it seemed only an outer expression of my inner pain. I never went for help until much later in the evening when my father and stepmother came home, even though my arm was a mass of blisters and open angry flesh. The accident seemed no more and no less than all of life itself, simply an outer expression of inner truth.

One redeeming constant during those years was a spiritual relationship with the Blessed Virgin Mary; although the Catholic hierarchy has raised her to the status of a woman of uncorrupted matter (with the 1954 cannon decree that she was lifted to heaven by the angels, her body fully glorified), the Church maintains that she is not a deity.

I argue that for many Catholics she is the unconscious symbology of the Great Mother, the feminine face of God. We pray the rosary to her, believe that her son, Jesus, will deny nothing that she asks on our behalf, and honor and pray to her as one prays to God himself. Even within my devotion to her, sustained throughout my life, I experienced a deep conflict for many years following my mother's death.

To summarize the conflict, many of my Catholic neighbors believed that because she died in childbirth, my mother received a special dispensation in death; she was, according to our beliefs, taken directly to heaven. A belief that I understood and still do as a patriarchal entrapment of women. My mother had nine pregnancies. She was tired and also frail. Some years before her final and ninth pregnancy, and after the delivery of my sister Michelle, my mother had almost died. Yet she had two more pregnancies. My mother also was devoted to the Blessed Virgin and considered it an act of devotion to trust in her and her Son, and to avoid any but the "natural form" of birth control. For her, this was an expression of faith. I remember feeling angry that instead of claiming her own health she sat on a chair daily and prayed her devotional to the Mother, the rosary. Even with conflict and anger spilling into so much of my bereavement, I too continued to love the Virgin and to communicate with her.

I share all of this because the field in which this experience of the psychoidal realm occurred was one in which the Great Mother archetype broke through the bounds of my own consciousness. The excitement of all three archetypal experiences—death, the orphan, and the Great Mother—was far more than my personal psyche could contain; the psychic energy spilled into the imaginal field. As I will discuss later, the Great Mother archetype did not manifest as a projection of my psychic reality but did influence the visual form through which the psychoidal figure presented.

Thus, I share my affect and my state of mind because they both played a part in the manifestation of the figure that first night. One of several ways in which the imaginal field constellates is within a matrix of lowered consciousness, a state that often accompanies grief, loss, and unresolved conflict. Frequent experiences of reverie were occurring also, psyche's attempt to find meaning and healing.

Finally, my spiritual practice contributed to the constellating field. I went to Mass daily and received the Blessed Sacrament, a practice of mine long before and well after my mother's death. In my religious tradition, the act of receiving communion is a sacrament, a joining of our own humanity with the body and blood of Christ. For practicing Catholics, this is not a symbolic act but a mystery and a real taking in of His body and blood.

This act, like no other, has brought me on several occasions to an other-worldly state of being, and can best be described as a state of ecstasy and also an experience of the unus mundus, a state of one-ness with all of life.

Receiving communion was one of the very few aspects of life that had not been altered by the loss of my mother, my school, and my community. The sacrament of communion was a practice that remained sweet and satisfying, often followed by a state of consciousness in which I was spiritually and emotionally full and at peace. Although I do not and did not then consider myself a mystic and was a modern child of the 1960's who loved Elvis and screamed uncontrollably at the sound of the Beach Boys in concert, I also frequently entered this more esoteric experience of the divine.

## THE IMAGE-MAKING CAPACITY OF SOUL

All of this—my lowered state of consciousness, my spiritual devotion, my deep bereavement—not only constellated the imaginal field, but influenced the nature of my figure's subtle form. Both imaginal figures and wholly human participants in soulful encounters possess an organ of imagination. It allows for an experience of poesis, the Greek word for making; both the human psyche and the psyche of imaginal figures engage in this image-making capacity.

My figure's being held its own reality, yet her form, as opposed to her spirit-essence, was a constellation of my own imagination and hers. She appeared simply a woman; and yet, as I told in the story, she possessed a form much like the "Madonna in a Mexican procession" and, I might add, much like the statue of the Virgin I kept in my room. Her demeanor was much like that of my memory of my mother on that fateful morning when she held me and consoled me after I had the premonition dream; this kind figure who attempted contact for so many years, bent her head, as my mother had that morning. Her hands, too, were gentle and graceful, like my mother's. She was not my mother, nor was she the Blessed Mother, yet she borrowed certain image qualities from them, so that I might relate to her and know, if only at an unconscious soulful level, that her intention was toward love and illumination. Corbin (1997) describes such manifestations of spiritual figures as "thought forms that appear in mirrors" (p. 218), meaning that the angel like the one whose illumination I experienced exists within a mystic geography of the world. In her subtle state of immaterial matter, she wears the garments, or forms, of worldly and other-worldly figures (my mother and my constellated Blessed Virgin), including their contours and their colors.

My own world and that of the imaginal figure intersected when the excited archetypes within me—the archetype of death and the orphan archetype—broke through the bonds of my own psyche and affected the imaginal world just as a constellated field can affect matter, as it does in incidents of synchronicity. It is my view that within the spirit of the angel, an equally excited archetypal response spilled over. She and I, in the moment of her visitation, became the matter and spirit end of the same two archetypes, death and the orphan.

It is my sense that she did not just happen to be there by chance, that our two realms did not accidentally collide, but rather that an other influenced her toward the encounter and that she responded to its call, much as a human being can respond to a feeling or an intuition, thereby using her embodied nature to visit a lonely friend, to hear a story of grief, or to exercise an act of kindness. We were engaged in a phenomenon in which the psyche and matter mirror each other, and at the same time were held within a broader field of experience, a totality beyond either of us.

The exploration of this experience will not be complete without consideration of the delivery of the box. Delivery was the purpose of her visit. My goal was to prevent her from delivering it; this was based on a belief that to take the box would be profoundly overwhelming, perhaps even deconstructing. Both my decision not to accept her box and its contents, and her insistence on delivering it were, I believe, secondary to the actual experience of "breaking through" the realm in which we encountered each other.

The box, which she extended, was symbolic of the things she would bring to my experience—knowledge, connection, guidance, and internal structures. My associations to the contents of the box have remained consistent over time; they are linked to the flowers a girl receives at her first prom. They are special, a mark of her being poised at a turning point, and given by that which she is not, a counterpart of self. When the girl receives those first flowers, the gift is symbolic of her being taken to a new phase of life by one who chooses her. Had I been able to allow a relationship with my figure, she would have brought me knowledge about life, similar to that which my personal mother would have given me in my adolescent years and, because of her nature, knowledge beyond the personal. The box "of flowers" was a gift of illumination.

My relationship with her would have been much like Jung's (1961 / 1989) with Philomen. Of this quality of realness Jung writes, "Philomen represented a force which was not myself. In my fantasies, I held conversations with him, and he said things, which I had not consciously thought. For I observed clearly that it was he who spoke, not I" (p. 183).

Later, he described Philomen as an outer companion when he wrote, "At times he seemed to me quite real, as if he were a living personality. I went walking up and down the garden with him, and to me he was what the Indians call a guru" (1961 / 1989, p. 184). It was to Philomen that Jung gave credit for his knowledge of the reality of the psyche.

This same experience of the psychoidal was described by Russian psychiatrist, Kharitidi (1996) when she wrote in her memoir about the spirits who initiated her into shamanism and communicated with her afterwards. Of an expanded experience of reality, one spirit voice instructed her:

The psychological structure of each person will be transformed, because people's old model of reality will no longer be sufficient. Your people will experience and learn to understand another part of their being. This will happen differently for each person. For some it will be easy and almost instantaneous. Others will need to struggle through stress and pain. There will even be some people who will be so deeply grounded in your old laws of reality that they won't notice anything at all. (p. 162)

Because my own ego at the time of my angel's first visit was too undeveloped and was also compromised by grief, she seemed too terrible. My feelings for her are captured in Rilke's (1978) poem:

If the dangerous archangel
        took one step now
                down toward us
from behind the stars
        our heartbeats
                rising like thunder
would kill us. (p. 27)

Being in the midst of a deconstructed world at the loss of my mother accounted for both the angel's presence and my inability to engage her.

Her being "terrible" was not connected to ill intention, but to her being frightening due to my inability to accept the reality in which she existed.

One might consider on the surface that this was another loss. I do not. Having experienced this figure, as I did over many years, has changed my own understanding of reality. My relationship with the angel, although it has not flowered as it might have, isn't constricted by the same laws of time and space that govern more conventional relationships. There is still possibility. I am not even sure that she is gone, only that I am no longer haunted by her presence. And the gifts she would have given me, came, I believe, very slowly over time as I matured, healed, and engaged the world; those gifts entered my soul through other avenues of human experience.

Because she and I could communicate from the start, I know that she never required me to be inauthentic. Serving her ego, if she has one, was never part of our relationship. Her intention, to act out of her nature in light, was fulfilled and was not predicated on my ability to accept or reject her. For me, the greater gift is that we both did encounter each other and I was able to respond with conscious acknowledgement, a contribution greater than my fear. It is enough that after 49 years I am able to give voice to the experience, thereby fulfilling my intention that the encounter be publicly spoken, and therefore not be erased through time.

## MIRRORING INNER AND OUTER

There is an epilogue to this story. The apparition of my figure is an example of an archetypal constellation breaking out of the bonds of human experience and reaching into the imaginal realm of spirit–souls, to form a mirror expression of the same reality. I wish to describe a less complex but equally compelling example of psyche and matter expressing mirrored images. In my story, I wrote of my surprise and sense of wrongness that the sun rose each day after my mother died, as if all was normal in the world. I have friends who experienced a similar feeling after they have lost a parent: surprise that the natural world had not changed, experiencing too a sense of disharmony and disbelief at witnessing the playful gurgling of a brook, or the exuberant outburst of flowers on a mountain outcrop.

There is, in the experience of the unity of life, a need for a mirroring of inner and outer, a wish for material form to balance psyche, and conversely, for psyche to balance material form. For instance, I told in my

story that I felt as though I could not breathe in the months after my mother's death, a metaphor of the psychological experience that accompanies
each of life's losses for me. The sense of not getting air, of not being able
to breathe has become my soul's habit when faced with, what feels in the
moment, like unacceptable loss. I felt as if I couldn't breathe after my son's
death, and in the years following the departure of my second husband. In
those days I found myself repeating the phrase, "I feel like I'm breathing
sand."

With each loss, my body has responded with respiratory difficulties.
I have had pneumonia several times, long bouts with colds, and more serious bronchial conditions. And now, while I experience myself as a fit
and healthy woman who enjoys nature walks, walks a treadmill daily, and
weight trains regularly, there is a marked diversion from the picture of
health; I have a chronic asthma condition. To breathe and sleep comfortably I must take a daily dose of Advair, Fluticasone Propionate, Singular,
and Clariton. After years of an inner experience of not being able to find
enough air, psyche demanded a corresponding somatic expression, a mirrored condition so that balance could be present.

I do not view my asthma condition as pathology but rather as a kind
of scarring that, given my totality of life experience, is acceptable. Hillman (1983b) writes that psychotherapy's need to cure is not always wise.
He describes a tree that is scarred early in its development by a lightning
strike, yet continues to grow beautifully through the years. As its maturing
canopy encompasses a vast space, the strength and beauty of the tree ren-
der the physical scar only a small part of the whole, as much a mark of its
worthy life as its massive trunk and its varying shades of green. My asthma
is not a somatic pathology but a soulful expression of my life experience.
I have grown beyond the experience of loss, the moments of scarring, and
I like the tree, have grown abundant. The scar is a part of the wholeness,
even welcomed just as I welcome the bounty of my life.

CHAPTER TWO

# THE UNDERWORLD

In the two stories that follow, I explore the archetype of descent—that journey traveled by many—in which psychologically and spiritually, one is in unknown territory, a place that feels much like the dark forests in fairy tales. One is often frightened in those forests, feeling that danger lurks in the shadows, that the skills and talents one has in "normal" life do not apply, or worse, are useless. In both stories, imaginal figures ask to be revealed, to be personally encountered in those darker places of experience.

As you read my accounts your initial response may be, "These stories don't feel unusual, much less otherworldly, or under-worldly. I don't see hidden truths or imaginal figures. These stories are uneventful happenings in everyday life." I would ask you to hold that thought until you read further.

So many of our everyday experiences appear unremarkable until and unless we choose to be present to them—to wonder, to explore, to allow ourselves to look more deeply at the figures within the stories. It is in this act of careful regard that something else appears, that a tear in the fabric of the world, the normal world, opens. It is through this portal that we find illumination and sometimes transformation. Upon entering this soulful place, a place full of souls, the multitude of figures within our literal and imaginal stories, including our cultural and individual dreams, become enlivened.

I will do in this chapter what I have promised to do throughout this book, which is to share a snapshot of my life, including an account of my own beliefs and feelings about each event. I also share relevant ideas that shape the experience.

If you decide at some point to meet your own imaginal figures at deeper levels of your life experiences, then your own personal beliefs and feelings, as well as your ideas about your experiences, will bring the illumination that allows growth. This interaction of the personal and the imaginal is what transforms, what changes our hearts.

In the first story titled, "The Raptor," Iranian mysticism, with its notions on revealing the Hidden God, sheds light on a mutually enriching interaction between divinity and corporeal beings. A red-tailed hawk is more than he first appears, and my encounter with him becomes a path from failure to redemption.

In the second story titled, "I Am Inanna," I explore imaginal figures as aspects of interiority, and also focus on Jung's (1959/1990) *archetype of transformation*. This second archetype, or pattern of human experience, is also a descent into difficult and unknown regions of being. The archetype of transformation describes a process through which one is tumbled about like a stone being polished. During the process, one suffers through abrasive experiences until one is more developed, and therefore, psychologically more whole. For example, many cancer survivors report that though they have suffered great losses, and their lives have often been threatened, they have been transformed. Many say that, for them, the experience was a gift for which they are grateful.

## THE RAPTOR

From 1985 to 1993, I lived very close to the natural world in the Northern California mountains. For me, this was a time of renewal and preparation for the more difficult years to follow, when a hawk and I, both of us in a space of personal breakdown, would co-create a field in which that which is present, yet invisible in the sensible world, is rendered visible. In our imaginal field, the hawk and I know each other within a totality, a tender oneness. In the space of our encounter, this hawk reaches out to me; in his eyes is the pathos of the divine. I am able to respond with a depth of sympathy (a sharing of pathos), or compassion, thereby fulfilling the fate brought to us both.

This is a story, too, about a synchronicity of events, which centers around the life and death of creatures in the animal world. On the Sunday morning when I encounter the hawk, I am rushing towards my veterinarian's office with a small dying cat in my arms. In responding to these animals as I do in the story, my internal capacities of healing, redemption, and transformation unfold. The events of my own life, as well as my affects and response to the world, are intertwined with theirs. This story is about the sacred unity among all of life's beings. And so I begin.

I am an East Coast native, yet I lived for 8 years in a remote valley in the Great Basin area of California, near Mt. Shasta, in the foothills of the Coast Range Mountains. Before living in this high desert landscape, which is 5,000 feet in elevation, I would not have believed that a land so otherworldly existed. More civilized Californians considered our area to be "off the I-5 corridor" meaning that this region was "bypassed" by the great California Interstate Highway, by all that marks the California life most people envision.

Additionally, the series of valleys and low mountains between our home and the ocean rendered us cut off from the California scene. County services were scarce, as were people in general. The closest McDonalds was 45 miles away, beyond a mountain pass, in Oregon. Here is where my family and I lived with a small herd of Arabian and Peruvian Paso horses, where wild mustangs roamed freely, and each year after the last alfalfa fields were harvested, a herd of a hundred antelope grazed until the winter snows covered the ground. My husband and I would have our coffee at the west end of the house after our workday was over, and marvel at their closeness to us and their unusual grace. Bald eagles and red-tailed hawks were everyday visitors.

As our valley stretched as far as the eye could see, one had a sense of sharing a vast enchanted land. The blackness of the expansive night sky was punctuated with razor-sharp stars; the high desert air held little moisture, so even the coldest winter days seemed crisp and clean. The relative absence of pollution exaggerated the sun's illumination; therefore, no matter how low the winter mountain temperature, one was warmed by the sun's rays, feeling always pure and alive.

Walking was my meditation practice in those days. My wolf Kara and I would leave the house in the summer months like two wild things sniffing out the world: she, in search of any dead thing to roll in, I in search of the natural surprises awaiting my eager heart.

Kara and I never came home empty-handed or empty-hearted, always discovering a precious treasure, like an abandoned nest or a patch of morel mushrooms for me, and a decaying carcass for her. It disgusted even my wild nature to have her drag rotting body parts home, yet that was as much her pleasure as the nests and mushrooms were mine.

One of my greatest "finds" was an experience while sitting under a ponderosa pine on an abandoned logging trail. The world and I were still; I was lost in the canopy of natural beauty that enveloped me when what felt like a thunderous expansion of air and sound, snapped me to attention in time to look above to see a great horned owl roused, I supposed, from her own pleasures by our intrusion. She spread vast wings that seemed to encompass the world, then as quickly as she announced her presence, she vanished, leaving me breathless, the air shuddering overhead.

Kara was totally disoriented, not knowing whether to throw me to the ground and cover me with her body, which was her enthusiastic custom on those rare occasions when she suspected that I was in danger or, to leap into the empty air in hot pursuit. As quickly as the moment came, it was done, leaving us both instinctually and incredibly alive, and I at least, full with gratitude that the world was good.

This life from 1985 to 1993 is where I revived my child's heart that had become constricted after my mother's death many years before. It was in those good years that I reconnected with the imaginal realm as it and I both flourished in the many joys of the natural world.

After 8 enchanted years, my idyllic landscape, both within and without, was ruptured after my husband lost his job and the warmth and containment of our marriage began dissolving. It was then, in the summer of 1993, that our family moved to California's dry and dusty Central Valley.

With so many stories of breakthrough of the imaginal world, there is first a moment of breakdown of the sensible and reasonable world. For me the truest image of life at that time of breakdown (which lasted for several years) was one that called to me from a compelling painting, which I impulsively and intuitively purchased. Its beautiful image reminds me of the rich cycles of life. It is aptly titled, "Shipwreck."

In the painting, a woman stands on the shores of what seems to be the rocky Maine coastline, her costume revealing an 18th century setting. As the violence of a storm whips her skirts and her long, full hair, her gaze is riveted to a nearby wooden ship as it is mercilessly crashed upon the unforgiving coastal rocks. My unconscious wanted me to buy that painting because the woman's story was my story. Both of us were caught in a violent storm that would deconstruct our lives. Just being able to look at her brought a deep resonance of the truth of my ruptured marriage, a truth too raw to be consciously known by me at that early time.

The red-tailed hawk and I encountered each other when Kara and I were living alone, "shipwrecked" in the low central part of the state. We were both homesick for the high desert of northern California and the wild freedom we found there. Fortunately, the instinctual sensibility that we had enjoyed there came to the lowlands with us.

A vast system of canals threads the desert terrain, providing irrigation for crops and also a natural habitat for marsh and red-tailed hawks. Those birds look so small as they soar long distances from the human eye, yet up close they weigh as much as newborn babies, their immense talons fully capable of eviscerating large jackrabbits.

Kara missed the freedom that roaming wild had given her, and hated the stifling desert heat. Her options to explore were so very limited, and as she was becoming older, I allowed her inside each evening to sleep on the floor beside my bed, pretending that I did not know that she roamed the house at night ferreting out and mauling the many wild finds that made my nature collection: rattlesnake skins, abandoned heron eggs, even a 15-year-old mounted quail given to me by a friend.

During this time, I was leading a professional development initiative in the school district near my home, and serving as a 4-year cat sitter, while my daughter pursued her college work in Manhattan, New York. Inwardly, I was devastated that my husband had ended our marriage. I was also attempting to adjust to the absence of my daughter. It's fair to say that I was hanging on by the thinnest of threads, often overwhelmed and fearful.

One evening, as part of a regimen of household chores, I meant to give Q-Tip, the cat, her dose of flea medicine, a small vial of oily medication rubbed lightly on the back of her neck. Instead, because I was lost to myself and thus lost to my responsibility to care for this precious being, I grabbed Kara's medication, meant for a 95-pound canine. While the vial appeared similar to Q-Tip's, the actual dose was large enough to overwhelm the cat's central nervous system and kill her.

Through the night, as I slept, Q-Tip suffered with violent convulsions. The next morning, as I raced her to the vet, I noticed the red-tailed hawk perched majestically on the two-lane highway. In front of him lay a bloody dead rabbit. I was somewhat puzzled that the hawk did not fly away as my car approached and buzzed past. Yet, I admit hardly caring, because the sweet cat that I had so mightily failed was still convulsing in the crook of my arm. Q-Tip was all I could think about then.

One hour later, as I returned from the veterinarian's office, relieved that the cat had not died and that a competent and caring vet was ministering to her, I was surprised to find the hawk in the same spot on Arroyo Road. I was struck too that his proud, still, attitude had not shifted in the hour since we first encountered each other. Pulling off the road, I rolled down my window, as if to ask a fellow traveler if I might help.

The hawk, so very large at this close distance, his chest held high, simply lifted his eyes and looked into mine with the clearest intention, meeting my gaze like a king. His expression, like none other I had seen before, allowed both of us to flow into the soul of the other. In that magical moment, there was no difference between human and animal, except that he was somewhat above me on an unseen hierarchy, as he presented himself for help. Although this connection lasted for seconds, at the same time, it felt like an eternity.

Finally, as if released from his gaze, I directed my attention downward. I saw a small pool of blood; clearly this was his blood and not the rabbit's. I understood then that an injury had prevented him from fleeing. I wondered if, as he deliberated upon his own work of eating, a vehicle, perhaps a high four wheeler, had hit and stunned him. It was a testimony to the necessity of our encounter, I believe, that he had remained undisturbed before and after I passed him on the road earlier that morning.

One would not normally try to lift a red-tailed hawk, its wingspan surprisingly large, its talons especially forbidding. Yet this creature would know, I realized, that I was trying to help him, and would assist me, just as in the past our very large injured or sick horses had known. However, I had not yet chosen to trust this idea. With the ending of my marriage, I found myself in a personal place of unrest, a condition that often causes our deeper wisdom to become muted.

It was at this moment that two men in a pickup truck stopped to wonder at the hawk's plight. "Looks like a car hit him when he went after the rabbit."

"Will you help me lift him," I inquired.

"You better call the sheriff's office or the chippies," they said. They meant the California Highway Patrol.

"I have to help him. Sometimes they don't respond for hours." I realized later that just as the men were afraid to trust the hawk, I was afraid to trust any system bound by human rules or laws.

Reaching for my cell phone, I called the vet for help, knowing he would still be in his office, attempting to save Q-Tip, washing off the debris of the poison, giving her Valium to calm the convulsions. "Sure," he said, "bring him in; I'll do what I can."

The men drove on, shaking their heads at my foolhardy decision to lift a wild creature that had never smelled human scent up close. I remember my irritation at their silly white cowboy hats and great silver belt buckles. I realized later that had they chosen at least to watch for passing cars as I did my work, I would have experienced their dress as charming and authentic.

I chose to trust that this suffering creature had asked for help, and in the way of heart, I knew that he would not attack, knowing my intentions as I knew his. As I lifted him, a strange feeling overcame me, a sense that I was also lifting myself. I would realize later that the hawk's situation mirrored my own internal world. I also was rendered stunned and in need of help in those days, experiencing myself as wounded and suddenly incapacitated while going about the business of life's daily work.

I remember the unusual weight of his body; it was "dead weight." I glanced too at the bleeding rabbit, which had been the bird's meal about an hour before. He too was sent into the underworld, without warning, in the midst of life's work. In all four of us that day—the cat, the hawk, the rabbit, and I—the cycle of life and death was present.

When I reached the vet's office, we examined the raptor. What I thought would be a small wound turned out to be a shattered shoulder, the work, no doubt, of a shotgun blast. The vet administered antibiotics and said, "We have a raptor expert on staff; if the hawk survives the night, she'll perform surgery tomorrow." Thankfully, he did not share that he believed that the hawk had as much chance for survival as my cat, which was very little.

Mercifully, Q-Tip did survive, although we would not know that for several days. In the vet's experience, none as sick as she had survived before. A team of remarkable veterinarians and their assistants worked on her for days, while she moved again and again into convulsions each time the valium wore off; the vets would extract bloody urine, knowing that this was symptomatic too of her grave condition. The game plan was to keep her calm and alive as her little body attempted to process the poison.

I came in after work each day and lay on the floor beside her open cage, on a horse blanket that an assistant always prepared for me. In a rhythmic movement, I would bring my hand several inches above her body, moving it from her head to tail, being careful not to disturb her material body. In a shamanic ritual, I worked to heal the energy above and within her, which I knew was a central part of her being. I gently encouraged her and communicated love and healing. One day, the vet who owned the clinic, a kind and wise medical man, stood above me and observed. After some time, he said in a respectful and sober tone, "You're healing her." It was as much a question as an observation.

I looked up at him, and simply said, "Yes," and continued on. That was the beginning and end of any conversation about my own part in the work. I would always be grateful that no one in the team ever blamed me for the stupid act of poisoning this little creature (although the blame was mine), and that they allowed space in their world of medical procedures for an older kind of healing work.

I too would survive those difficult and disorienting days. Sadly, my raptor would not. Yet, what was necessary in our encounter was that he would communicate his need for help and compassion, and I would listen and do my part, not leaving him, as if he were nothing, on the road to die. I remember vividly the warmth of his willing body as I lifted him to my car and the union that my embrace brought to us both. We were called together for that joining, a recognition of a unity which once was. Because we were one, in responding to each other we became participants in a mystery.

This encounter was what Jung (1960/1984) describes as a synchronicity, a meaningful coincidence in which an inwardly experienced event is seen to have a correspondence in external reality. Those small creatures mirrored the psychic reality of my own shipwrecked life. Although I could not give verbal expression to these events at the time, I knew that this was no ordinary moment, and I understood that a thin veil of the world had been parted. I knew too that the wounded hawk in the road was also an opportunity for redemption for me.

To explain this attitude linking redemption to these events, I need to tell the one part of my story that remains in the shadows. In the dark hours of the morning, before I found Q-Tip convulsing on the floor, I was awakened from sleep by a violent crashing against my bedroom door. I was frightened then, as I often was in that difficult time. For me, just waking from sleep, the noise seemed overwhelming, like disembodied violence and also a terrible demand from the elemental world. Cowering in my bed, reminded that I was alone, I, like the child I had become in the moment, hoped that whatever made the noise would simply disappear. From that unseemly perspective I, admittedly a grown professional woman, literally covered my head with blankets and hid.

To my horror, in the morning, upon seeing Q-Tip helpless and near death, her tiny, pink tongue hanging from her pathetic mouth, I realized that it was she who had thrown herself against my door, repeatedly and desperately, begging for assistance.

The landscape of the underworld is not marked by the rising and setting of the sun, but by the comings and goings of things that lurk in the dark hours of night, in other words by those imaginal realities that become grotesquely animated when the ego's presence fades. What lay between my cat's cries and a more timely intervention that dark night was my own fear. Thus, as I returned from the vet and encountered the bird, I was fully aware that I had gravely failed one innocent being that day and was being given another opportunity to redeem both of us.

In the encounter on the road, while my heart confirmed that the raptor would help me assist him, my rational mind warned that his instincts would force a confrontation; I worried that I risked my own well-being, perhaps my eyesight in trying to lift him. Yet, in the moment when I raised him from the ground and felt his body release into my own good intention, I knew that psyche had brought him to me, a second chance to respond.

What eluded me until much later was that the hawk mirrored my own fragile, wounded soul, and when I found the courage and strength to follow the whispers of the in-between world on his behalf, I had turned a corner toward bringing myself back to life. That was the sacred moment when I began the work of regaining my center, the moment when the paralysis of abandonment became leavened by the strength of the uniqueness of Self.

You may be wondering, "How is this story of the hawk a visionary encounter?" To answer this question I turn first to the wisdom of Iranologist Henry Corbin whose words illuminate the encounter between the hawk and me on that California road. He offers insight into a mystery between a Divine Other who wants to be known and the beings who know Him or Her. Second, I offer, in the following section titled "Shattered Shoulder and Burnt Wing," insights from Eric Neumann's exploration of Divine union in his analysis of the myth of Psyche and Amor. Third, Neumann's understanding of the development of feminine consciousness, which is

synonymous with the development of soul, brings yet another lens with
which to understand.

The final and most relevant answer to the question is my experience
during and after the encounter with the figure of the hawk. Though my
own experience weaves in and out of every section of this book, I will
summarize personal thoughts relative to this particular story in which I
describe changes within me and how they manifest in affects, attitudes,
and behaviors.

## DIVINE SYMPATHY AND COMPASSION

For Corbin (1997/1998), visionary experiences are "…those acts in which
human beings are conscious of penetrating into another world" (p: 120).
In exploring the encounter I draw from esotericism, because although my
soul understands what occurred when I encountered the hawk, communicating about it is difficult due to the soulscape's lack of abstract language
and reason. Corbin (1998) acknowledges this difficulty, yet provides useful concepts with which to describe such events. Notably, he draws from
Iranian theosophy the idea of the descent of the Divine and simultaneous
ascent of less evolved spiritual beings toward the realization of each other
in the act of union, a phenomenon that is central to the understanding of
my story. The term phenomenon here is used in the spiritual sense, meaning that the experience, while remaining veiled, reveals itself.

In explaining this Divine nature, Bamfield (Corbin, 1998) describes
a Divinity who in sympathy and passion is bound to the spiritual essence
of humanity, a Divinity who comes into being as she/he is experienced.
He says:

> The Hidden God becomes a Revealed God by virtue of another
> essential polarity, namely, the polarity of "passion" and "sympathy."
> That is, there is a divine passion, a conversion or tropos, toward
> spiritual humanity, to which corresponds precisely and freely a
> human, theopathic, theotropic sympathy.
>
> The human being and God are bound together, as inner and outer
> are, by passion and sympathy; and spiritual knowledge (ta'wil, prayer)
> is but the conjugal Arcanum, the secret rhythm of reciprocity. The
> Divinity seeks a being whose God He is, to which we respond. It is by

our theopathy that we constitute him as God." Thus, the fundamental ground again becomes an essential bi-unity, an unus-ambo, a dialectic between each being and his Lord an unio sympathetica whose expression is love. (P. LVI)

My response to the hawk with a spirit of sympathy (union) and shared suffering, as well as appreciation of his sacred entitlement, became an act of reaching up, or ascent. The Divine also experiences the essential polarity between sympathy (union) and passion (as in shared pathos), thereby creating the transformation among beings, including that of the Divine (Corbin, 1998). In the book titled Answer to Job, Jung (1991) more fully explores this dynamic in which the Divine seeks a meeting with lower spiritual consciousness for his or her being to be realized.

As the raptor and I, each within the limits of our capacities, entered an understanding of the Divine, we participated in a passion, a pathos that is lived and shared with the understood God. For me this participatory act began at the moment when I chose to lift the hawk and take him for treatment. It was then that we more deeply entered the inner world in the field of soul.

I can only describe the subsequent union and revelation as I experienced it, which for me constituted entering the presence of my true self, what Bamford (Corbin, 1998) describes as "my true I, who is a spiritual, angelic being at home in a spiritual, angelic world" (p. xxiv). To be in the presence of one's true Self is what is meant, at least in this particular biographical incident, by Divine union.

It is consciousness that brings forth the revelation that one is in another dimension. In the story, I experienced this revelation as the moment in which I "found my center" and began to reenter the world after a long period of psychological descent. This also was an experience of Jung's transcendent function, a moment in which the ego and the unconscious met, resulting in a resonance, and a shift in gnosis.

To experience such a moment consciously is complex because as I reflect on this particular visionary encounter, there was first a period in which my soul was aware, causing me to experience myself as full, light filled, richer; the sense of aloneness vanished. However, this soul gnosis is deep and not easily discerned by the ego. I can only liken it to first moments of recovery from prolonged grief, in which joy comes quietly and like a butterfly rests softly for a brief moment on one's shoulder and flies away, to return intermittently.

Over time, the moments of joy seem to stay longer, and much later, after healing is complete, joy becomes part of one, easily allowing soulful and exuberant animations, much like the one described in the earlier "Coffee Hour" story. Thus, this early and somewhat intermittent soul consciousness of union with the Divine was followed by an ego consciousness in which I made the connection between that sense of abundance and the sacred presence in the experience itself.

How did the hawk and I enter this illuminating dialectic between inner and outer (the hawk's descent to the underworld and his mortal wound/my own descent and redemption through reaching out to him)? Our encounter held an invitation by the hawk: for me to know him as more than a beast. When I stopped at the side of the road, the hawk's gaze penetrated my soul, filling it with the knowledge that he and I were brother and sister beings. We were attached in spiritual union that flowed from our shared state of pathos and sympathy. In this sense, the hawk and I were "like" acting on "like," meaning that any hierarchical division of human and sentient beast had dissolved.


## SHATTERED SHOULDER AND BURNT WING

Divine union is also described in the myth of Psyche and Amor (Eros), in which the Divine (Eros) meets the soul of the mortal (Psyche) in nightly passionate trysts.

In Neumann's (1971) hermeneutic treatment of the Psyche myth, Soul (Psyche) wins consciousness as she illuminates the sleeping god Amor. However, when he is burned by the oil, which spills from the lamp, he awakes from sleep; both human and god become conscious. Psyche's burning of Amor's wing symbolizes that one pays a price for consciousness. Though Psyche discovered the truth of her lover's identity, the price she paid was loss of mystery and him. He, at least for a time, lost her.

For me, to lift the hawk brought forth the face of the Divine as She joined with us to reveal her concealed self. The hawk's shattered shoulder, like Amor's burnt wing, was the wound that accompanied the transformation from the hidden to the revealed.

It is worth noting that the material world mirrors the spirit end of the archetype. We see this mirroring in the Amor and Psyche myth: Psyche's object of love was a beast (the material end of the archetype), seen as a beast until the moment of illumination revealed him to be a god (the spirit end of the archetype). In my story the hawk too was both a kindly beast and a vehicle for Divine manifestation. The price required of me for consciousness of the Divine presence was movement through fear toward reunion with the angel within. The hawk of course lost his material existence, but not before his sacred participation in the phenomenon was fulfilled.

Significant also to the events of the story is the link between my earlier opening to the natural world—as experienced in long walks, relationships with my own horses, the antelope herd, and the close bonding between my Mexican Red Wolf and myself—and the figure of the hawk that Psyche brought for the encounter. (Here I use the term Psyche in its broader sense).

My early experiences of the elemental, or natural, world created in me a soulful belief system in which beasts and the earth herself were members of a vibratory, relational universe of beings. The world and all her creatures had souls as I experienced them and while I could not rationally converse with them I could feel their dynamic dignity and worth.

I understood that just as I, a human soul, glorified the Divine by simply being, the creatures of the earth also sang hymns of praise. This ability of all earthly beings, each within individual limitations of power, to greet the Divine in prayer is beautifully expressed by Proclus, the last of the Greek Platonists in Corbin (1997):

> What other reason can we give for the fact that the heliotrope follows in its movement the movement of the sun and the selenotrope the movement of the moon, forming a procession within the limits of their power, behind the torches of the universe?
>
> For, in truth, each thing prays according to the rank it occupies in nature, and sings the praise of the leader of the divine series to which it belongs, a spiritual or rational or physical or sensuous praise; for the heliotrope moves to the extent that it is free to move, and in its rotation, if we could hear the sound of the air buffeted by its movement, we should be aware that it is a hymn to its king, such as it is within the power of a plant to sing. (1933, pp. 102–106)

Unity with the Divine in prayer, the act of ascending toward, as explained by Proclus, allows one to be engaged by the essence of a beast, whom one experiences as a brother. In the same fashion, a beast can also choose, to the extent that it is free to choose, to participate in Divine mystery—just as the heliotrope follows the movement of the sun. I maintain that just as I chose to respond to the hawk and his communication with me, he too made a choice. I know, to a small extent, his quality of consciousness, because for the brief moment in time that the experience unfolded, he and I shared a field of being, a shared consciousness in an in-between world.

## THE ELEMENTARY AND TRANSFORMATIVE FEMININE

Neumann's (1954/1983) understanding of the elementary and transformative character of feminine consciousness points to an additional layer of relatedness between the beast and human. Elementary and transformative are terms Neumann uses to describe the early and later stages in the maturation of feminine capacities in both men and women, meaning that these terms are used to describe the development of soul.

The earliest quality of feminine consciousness, the elementary character, is not differentiated and is symbolized by the circular snake biting its tail and is referred to as the Great Round, or uroboros. The elementary character of the feminine, like the Great Round, tends to hold fast to everything that springs from it and to surround it. Neumann (1954/1983) writes that everything born of it belongs to it and remains subject to it. "Even if the individual becomes independent, the Archetypal Feminine relativizes this independence into a nonessential variant of her own being (p. 25)."

Important to the story is the notion that the elementary character of the feminine becomes evident whenever the ego and consciousness are small and undeveloped, and the unconscious is dominant. This state was true for me, especially in the early part of the encounter as well as in the months before. I experienced myself as lost, alone, frightened, a train derailed (this described the hawk's situation also).

The image of the ship, described early in the "Raptor" story, crashing against the coastal rocks is symbolic of my ego state at the time of the encounter with the hawk: fragmented, relativized, and fragile. In such a state, which can be characterized as borderline, the hawk and I could experience a merged consciousness.

Neumann's (1955/1983) idea supports this notion when he writes that the elementary character of the feminine is ambiguous and relativized and that in a tension between ego and the unconscious there exists a tendency of the ego to return to its original unconscious state. This elementary character of the feminine can be seen as the indissoluble state between the mother and infant—psychic life is predominantly static, all processes of transformation lead back to the original situation from which they arose. The infant and mother are one, much like the uroboros whose beginning and end are the same.

The function in which the elementary character operates is to nourish and protect, to keep warm and hold fast. The events of the story titled "The Raptor" describe such a function and support my claim that the elementary character of the feminine is the state in which the hawk and I shared our experience. We were indissoluble; we entered an interactive field in which the unconscious manifested and was mutually encountered.

Ego and consciousness may be impaired or altered by constellations such as fatigue, sickness, prolonged grief, or as in my memoir, a life in utter breakdown. Although there is a tendency in psychology to equate such a movement toward a dissolved ego to states of pathology, I claim that esoteric encounters require fluidity and are not pathological states. I maintain that in this particular esoteric encounter between the hawk and me, there is a dance between the elementary character of the feminine and the transformative character.

While the elementary character tends to dissolve the ego and consciousness in the unconscious, the transformative character of the feminine sets the personality in motion, produces change, and ultimately transforms (Neumann, 1954/1983).

The archetype most commonly associated with the transformative character is the anima. For a man, the encounter with the anima initiates a change in the relation of the ego to the unconscious as well as of the man to a woman. The action of the unconscious also assumes new and creative forms. For a woman, an encounter with the anima, or the transformative character of the feminine, results also in growth of ego in relationship to the unconscious. To use one of Neumann's examples, a woman in whom the transformative character is dominant would cease to be an unconscious vehicle of feminine development in her mate; rather, she would realize the anima in herself.

Thus, her relationship to her mate would become predominant and conscious; she would begin engaging in a more genuine relationship. Neumann (1954/1983) writes, "The woman in whom the transformative character is dominant represents a higher, or rather later stage of development" (p. 36). In seeing the hawk as a valued, sentient individual, I was beginning to realize my anima, my own soul. The hawk was not an archetypal beast in our moment of mutual experience, but a unique being with whom I was relating.

As conscious encounters with the anima result in a change in the relation of the ego to the unconscious, my own encounter with the hawk brought illumination, an experiential understanding of the rhythms of descent.

## PERSONAL BELIEFS AND AFFECTS IN THE IMAGINAL FIELD

The work of illumination requires a spiritual hermeneutic, a quest to uncover that which is concealed behind the symbolic. As I attempt to demonstrate that the imaginal realm is at work in every life, and to argue that one need not be an esoteric initiate to encounter this realm, the central challenge is to communicate the realities of this realm through rational dialogue. To be as clear as possible, it is useful to speak in terms of my own experience of the phenomenon itself.

As I have said in my story, I was in a time of "shipwreck." It is important to underscore that it is in moments of breakdown of the physical or psycho-spiritual world that moments of breakthrough occur. From the outside, I was simply a woman whose husband had left, whose only child had gone to school 3,000 miles away, and who found herself in a new community with few friends.

But it was more than that in terms of inner psychological experience. It was a breakdown of a life, my life. I am psychically allergic to loss, having experienced too many previous deaths of loved ones, both too early in my development and too close together.

I believed then that my husband was my soul mate. What this means to me now is that I projected much of my inferior function and light shadow aspects onto him. By this I mean that I wasn't able at that time to live fully, securely, joyfully, or confidently out of my own talents, my own developed self. (Light shadow refers to a positive aspect of self that has not been realized consciously.)

It was as if my soul voted to leave me and dwell in him, such that when he left, he seemed to take my soul with him. Thus, I experienced myself as soulless, perhaps the most desolate, nihilistic state in which I've dwelt. It was essential to my psycho-spiritual health that I not remain stuck in that painful place. Therefore, finding a portal to the *mundus imaginalis*—where the Divine shared sympathy and compassion with the hawk and me, shared Her Being, and needed us both, to experience Her own unfolding—was a sacred gift.

In the hours and days that followed my encounter with the hawk, ego consciousness developed as a sense of fullness, a righting of the shipwreck. For instance, my sense of being in relationship with the self allowed me to go to the veterinary clinic day after day and perform shamanic healing rituals on my small cat, an act which I would not have done earlier because I would not have possessed the necessary moral authority.

My encounter with the hawk was a lived phenomenal reality, that of being in the moment of revelation. This is modern esotericism, which I claim has taken its position on the cusp of societal consciousness, available for discovery by others who chose to wonder about life's deeper mysteries, choose to be soul singers, and choose to listen to Psyche's whispers. What is required is openness to a reality before and beyond Cartesian thought.

Psychologically, I ask my reader to consider, in experiences such as the one cited in this chapter, fluid and complex states of consciousness as part of the imaginal experience, moving toward a cautious acceptance of borderline states as helpful and not problematic. When states of ego consciousness become less differentiated and are also mediated by meaning-making capacities, they need to be understood as providing opportunities to opening one to the in-between world of the *mundus imaginalis*.

## PROLOGUE TO I AM INANNA

The next story, titled "I Am Inanna" is the one in which I found my sacred, instinctual being, allowing me to live a woman's life, belonging to no one, and contained by no patriarchal order. Psychologically and spiritually I have returned from this, a second round of my descent journey with a sense of gratitude.

Without the containment of the many imaginal figures who accompanied me along the way, my story might well have had a different ending. These figures were not all the same. Some allowed me to approach mystery. This is what occurred when, in a particularly difficult time, I called out to a Divine Other.

Another figure, the Grand Canyon, became soul's metaphor for the extraordinary process that allowed me to know, imaginally, what Jung (1959/1990) spoke of when he described the archetype of transformation, a pattern of human experience that is not a personality, but can move with the speed of a dream or, as in my story, with the current of years. Because I was able to maintain a degree of relationship with all of the imaginal figures that manifested, my ego was prevented from being overwhelmed by the deep demands of the experience.

Very often psyche brings us figures representing an internal personality, an unconscious attitude, which needs to become conscious if development is to continue, a difficult task in light of the ego's ferocious fight to maintain its positions. For example, in my story, my ego believed that I needed to reunite with my husband, that he was in the grip of a breakdown, and that he needed me to believe in him, to wait for him to return to our home. My unconscious, seeing something much different, brought me many dream images, telling me that it was I who needed care, and I who needed to find connection with my inner life force.

The reason that I am compelled to write this story is, as I have said earlier, a desire to learn about the ways in which imaginal figures interact with themselves and me. It is also my hope that my story might redirect the prevalent societal voice that blames and marginalizes women who, on the surface, allow and invite abuse, abandonment, and betrayal. Though that willing participation is indeed true to an extent, what is not so obvious is that the culture in which women live, provides many early experiences, which in effect set the stage for us to participate in future victimizations. Some of these are cultural traps that have been thoroughly exposed in feminist literature. But alas, all too quickly, the lessons learned, sink into the silence of the societal unconscious. In my particular situation there were two earlier events that I'll share later, which led to my vulnerability. My contribution is to provide more awareness, more consciousness, regarding the imaginal element playing out in abandonment situations.

# I AM INANNA

As my story begins, it is 1998, 17 years ago. I am working as a professional development leader in the California public schools and completing my doctoral studies in a clinical psychology program with an emphasis in depth psychology. The rhythms of my life combine a way of being, which includes daily dream work, spiritual practice, and therapy with a Jungian-oriented psychologist. In this story, it makes sense that these several perspectives contribute to a writer's voice that uniquely informs my day-to-day life.

My husband of 13 years, a man I mistakenly see as my soul mate, has disappeared into the Arizona Desert. The circumstances of his disappearance are not the subject of this story. It is enough to say that, in my experience, I am a woman abandoned, frightened, deeply confused, and in those initial days, burdened by a shame that is not mine.

Though I am a woman in my fifties, an inner, and unconscious, wounded girl child seems to fragment internally as the slow realization emerges, that my husband is not returning. I feel her young aspect of self in terrifying feelings in the night, in frequent feelings of deep loss and disorientation, as well as a sense of loneliness almost too painful to admit. It is at this point in my life that a descent to an underworld experience begins.

In her illuminating book, *Uncursing the Dark*, Betty de Shong Meador (1994) writes these timely words, "The problem for women who are trying to foster and nourish a wounded girl child is that the child ultimately must be grounded in the feminine instinctual aspect of Self" (p. 54), an aspect often expressed in intuitive wisdom, psychic healing, even proud sexuality. Later in the story, I'll tell about the moment when my own girl child, so bravely and poignantly, presents herself to me during an active imagination encounter.

The imaginal figures, which come in dreams, myth, and active imagination, loyally assist me, as I come to terms with a profound abandonment, a reality which my conscious ego tries to deny. This recurring, archetypal experience is something I need to embrace if I am to survive. At some level I seem to know this.

What I cannot seem to wrap my mind or soul around in these difficult months and years is that I am entering a transformative initiation rite. My descent to this underworld experience becomes the sacred path to my woman's life, in which I will own the entirety of my feminine voice, my body, and my desires.

When we find ourselves in the underworld, in the experience of descent, there are tests and crucial turning points during which we are aware that death (disintegration) and life (transformation) are close at hand. This experience, because it is what Jung termed archetypal, recurs over many cultures and over long periods of time. It is not surprising that it has found mythopoeic expression in the beautiful Sumerian myth of goddess Inanna in 3500 B.C.

I am uniquely fortunate because as my own descent journey rampages through my life, my doctoral studies are bringing me rich material, which speaks to my situation. From Meador I learn that the goddess Inanna, Queen of Heaven and Earth, descends to the depths to find herself brutally encountered by her sister Ereshkigal. Though Inanna suffers at the hands of her sister, it is in the depths of the experience that she finds her sacred and powerful identity. I begin to realize that I am mightily, though unconsciously, resisting the reality that Inanna's (and also my) drama is a primordial transformation story, one whose essential reality offers modern women a myth for liberation from the dismembering dynamic of a patriarchal order.

As a psychotherapist today, I am able to use my own descent experience to go into a chaotic and deep terrain with my patients. I am not afraid because I have been there before. For some patients, I am able to hold the attitude of Ereshkigal, Inanna's sister who participated in her initiation experience, insisting that Inanna let go of her naïve cultural views.

I remember two dreams from that frightening period. For me, fundamental shifts occur as I see through several dream images to the archetypes that reside within. It is in the "seeing through" that leads the way to my gradual healing. Therefore, I wish to share the images that I encountered during this period of descent as well as my understandings of them.

Dream 1
I am in my home, a glass skyscraper, which is caught in the violence of a tornado. I know that my husband has gone and mysteriously has not returned. I am alone as the tornado first lifts then dashes my children, my glass house, and me to the ground. We are screaming as we see the ground rushing toward us. I wake moments before impact. (Harrell, Dream Journal, 1998)

Through associations, turning the images around, and asking questions, I experience the following understanding of the dream figures:

Dream 1
The glass house feels like my fragile and brittle ego. Many of my organizing structures have disappeared. In the same month as my husband's abandonment, my only child left, as planned, to attend a 4-year university 3,000 miles away. Without familiar family patterns, I am constantly anxious and depressed. I am terrorized by feelings of loss of control, deep loneliness, and a state of mind, which is symbolized by the children in the dream who are dashed to the ground by the tornado. They are younger aspects of my own psychology that have been constellated during this difficult time. I continue to work at my demanding and rewarding position in professional development for my school district. This professional stability keeps me somewhat psychologically organized and distracted, and helps strengthen an ego under siege. The dream however is a reminder that my outer and inner worlds are dangerously out of balance. (Harrell, Dream Journal, 1998)

Dream 2
I am a yellow rose, which has been cut from its roots and lies at the floor beside my bed. The rose waits beside an intricately carved coffin under the bed. My husband lies in the coffin like Osiris, waiting to be brought back to life. My Mexican Red Wolf, Kara waits next to me keeping sentry over both of us. (Harrell, Dream Journal, 1998)

Dream 2
I am the yellow rose, which has been cut from my roots as I have been cut from what I mistakenly experience to be the source of my nourishment (my husband). Roots ground a rose to the earth where natural functions of stability and growth occur. The dream rose has no grounding, no strength. I later came to see this particular rose as a symbolic image of loss of instinctual life. I, the rose, am in an imaginal relationship with an absent husband. Because I have entered the relationship split off from my own feminine, I am moving toward the death instinct. (Harrell, Dream Journal, 1998)

There is more to the interpretation of these dreams, but for this current discussion I will stop here.

To interact with the imaginal figures in dreams is to find the reality of the unconscious. One does this by putting the dream stories to paper, wondering what the images are saying, noticing the accompanying affects, and asking for associations to the images. To recognize the depth, fullness, richness of psyche, that it has content, is to prevent a leaking out of soul life. For me, to link my own experience to the dream images provides some degree of healing and a sense of connection to solid ground.

Paradoxically, while the healing process is moving forward, I continue to deny the reality that my husband is gone and will not return. For years, I have hope that his voice is on the other end of every ringing phone, experiencing a sinking feeling in my stomach when the voice I hear belongs to someone else. This being "love sick" is a source of embarrassment and deep disappointment in myself, because intellectually I know that I am dependent and needy. This kind of conflict between what one knows, and how one feels and behaves is not unusual when in the throes of a complex.

What I cannot see, until later in time is that in the many years following this experience, I would be able to have more compassion for, and understanding of, who I was at that point in life. I would be able to hold a more patient attitude with my patients in similar dependent positions, when their points of view seem perplexing, or even preposterous.

For many months, I tell myself a fiction: that I should be "true" to my husband, to wait for him to change his mind in the face of my complete physical and emotional abandonment, because I "love" him. With this ego attitude, my own soul energy continues to diminish. I believe that he is deeply, emotionally wounded. Yet my understanding of the figure of the rose provides a different and trustworthy truth that I am without any source of soul nourishment and that my life, fragile as a glass high-rise, is careening in chaos. Psyche, in sending the dream, attempts to correct a problematic attitude that my ego position is completely "other focused," that is, husband focused, rather than self-focused. In other words, it would be far healthier for me to concern myself with my own more real and critical problem.

Additionally, as I study the timely words of Meador (1994), I now understand an image such as this tornado as the dark aspect of the feminine rising up in chthonic rage, a rage at my refusal to move toward a position of consciousness. Paradoxically, the tornado is also the image of wind/spirit (the masculine power principle) pointing to an overwhelming inner conflict. This angry pair, the inner masculine and feminine, is in an uproar, a result of my inability to act out of sense of agency, toward psychic life.

And lastly, the tornado as well as similar dream images in this time-frame—of flood, fire, and storm—also holds the symbology of an ego being overwhelmed. There is also some hope, as I am beginning to suspect, that this set of circumstances may be the raw material of my individuation.

## THE GIFT OF ERESHKIGAL, ANGRY SHADOW FIGURE

During the period in which I have these dreams, I continue to read Meador's book, *Uncursing the Dark*. Needless to say the Inanna myth within the pages speaks very personally to me, given my life situation. In Meador's words, the "myth tells an archetypal story of the primacy of the primordial, natural, instinctual feminine over the world of culture" (p. xi). Inanna's descent places the goddess into the realm of the dark, underworld feminine, where she meets the hungry greedy, ruthless goddess, Ereshkigal, her sister, who shakes her to the bones, demanding that Inanna let go of her narrow spectrum of desires, and her stunted vision of what life is and can be.

Feeling that Inanna's experience is also mine, I write the following words in a personal journal, words that at the time, I don't fully understand because they come from a soul place that has no past or future, and knows far more than my ego does:

> I shall always be awed that I survived my own days with Ereshkigal. She relentlessly screamed at me, that I was alone, without anyone to notice if I returned home at night. She was disgusted because I experienced abandonment as a slaughtering, felt annihilated and betrayed, and always, at some level, allowed terror to lay underneath my bed, in my dreams and in every waking moment. It was I, not Inanna, who was hanging from a meat hook, my flesh rotting and stinking of death. (Harrell, Personal Journal, 1998)

As I write these words, I haven't yet realized that in Ereshkigal's "personality" is a very deep voice within me saying, "Wake up."

I will come to know her later, as a gift, an unrealized (undeveloped) part of self who is angry and frustrated because I am naïve regarding so much that harms me, and childish in my inner response to the ending of my marriage. She knows, that for me to become whole, I need to let go of my fixed view, "If he abandoned me, he must be suffering." Unfortunately, my ego, the "I," didn't want to let go at all.

My inner Ereshkigal wants me to remember that a close friend of my husband had called me during that time telling me that people were gossiping, saying that my husband was involved with another woman. The friend even named her. I told him with the intransigency of my ego position that my husband would not do such a thing. I also refused to see classic signs of an affair that, in retrospect, filled every crevice and crack of our marriage. Years later, when my life would no longer be spinning, I would come upon a marriage certificate, showing that some months after I divorced my husband, he married the woman named in that phone conversation.

Like most shadow figures, when we acknowledge them, we often see, as I might have seen in the Ereshkigal figure that they have something worthy to offer: a different perspective, a more helpful attitude, or an appropriate impulse. They show up in our dreams, our fantasies, or our imaginings when we need them and when we are ready to integrate their attitude into our lives.

This is my time to allow Ereshkigal, ruthless in her common sense, into my personality. Unfortunately, that doesn't mean I don't continue to resist. I am holding the information that she knows, like a beach ball under the water, preventing it from surfacing. Like the beach ball kept under water too long, my unconscious contents are getting more difficult to keep below the surface.

## RETURN OF THE GIRL CHILD

A contributing early experience that leads to my inability to admit to myself that I am so alone during this time is, as my reader knows all too well, the early death of my mother in 1962 when I was 13. I became acutely aware, at that tender age, of the pain of the loss of a loved one.

It is not surprising that, in 1998, a 13-year-old imaginal figure manifests to help me understand that this younger aspect of me has become enlivened during this difficult time, and has decided, in the way of imagination, to weigh in on my positions and attitudes. Her ideas and her impulses, if left in the unconscious during this time, will not necessarily be helpful as she is so very young. What I mean is, by remaining in the unconscious, her immaturity and ignorance of the world of culture can keep me from a much needed emotional wellspring, that of the wise woman archetype.

Acknowledging her young presence, and feeling her very real feelings will help untangle my confused state of mind and my resistance to moving forward. The conscious encounter with her occurs one evening as I meet with my friend Sam who asks me why I continue to love a silent, rejecting partner. My answer doesn't make sense to anyone but me, "I love him and am committed to him. He is my husband and soul mate."

My wise friend, a therapist, though not mine, says, "There is another reason," and sits with me in silence. After some time, he repeats this, leaving me with the uncomfortable weight of his words, until I begin to *feel* what I can only describe as a diffuse ache somewhere in my body. Though the feeling resides in the body, I am able, by staying with the experience, to link this feeling to an unbearable sense of abandonment. Until that moment, the reality of abandonment, never having been named, lived subtly and unconsciously, in the soma, through a deteriorating asthma condition and a constant sense of emotional heaviness and physical lethargy.

Now, for the first time, I begin to fully, and consciously, experience my abandonment. In this moment I am so overwhelmed that literally I begin to writhe in pain. I feel a psychic pain also that moves like trapped lightening through my being, changing the experience of abandonment from a psychic to a physical one and back again.

Almost immediately, I imagine a 13-year-old child sitting on a bed, shoulders and back slumped in despair and shame, the shame of a motherless child who experiences herself as somehow at fault. This imaginal child, bereft at the knowledge that her mother was gone forever, is alone and unsafe in what seems like a vast and frightening world. This experience in the imaginal realm exemplifies Hillman's (1975) "seeing through" the image of the child, to the archetype of abandonment underneath.

It is this "seeing through" that informs me. The 13 year old has waited, for 37 years, to be embraced by an older Mary who at last could see her and know that she was alone and in need. It is with the help, the kindness, of Sam that I am able to tell the girl within that she is safe, loved, and worthy. This seeing through, and consequential shifting of psyche, only *begins* with the image. It will take many months of conscious moments in which the woman that I am in the present is able to reclaim, by thoughts, actions, and imagination, this split-off and abandoned girl child. This is a moment in which descent, transformation, and redemption seem to coalesce.

I continue very slowly to encounter other critical life experiences that had set the stage for me to abandon myself. I begin to understand how my early relationship with my father, who gave me life and a strong work ethic, but was also a wounded man, had caused me to give up my own reality as a child. This, along with my mother's sudden death, and my choice of husband all contributed to my loss of soul. All of these realities without the light of consciousness would contribute to an unreasonable state of "lovesickness."

Let's consider for a moment one cultural dynamic, which prepares young girls, if you will, for a pattern of abandonment. In a patriarchal society such as ours, abandonment of women wears a complex yet recurring face. It is often repetitive in nature, beginning with the setting of the stage in childhood. In her book *The Pregnant Virgin: A Process of Psychological Transformation*, Marion Woodman (1985) powerfully describes a scenario much like my own: "It occurs often as the girl child of a puer [psychologically undeveloped] father projects his own unfulfilled feeling values, his young anima, onto his little girl. The child is trapped in spiritual incest" (p. 35).

Woodman continues, describing how women abandon themselves as young girls:

> The daughter becomes spiritual mother, his beloved, his inspiration. If the father is not mature enough to value her for herself but forces her to become his star performer, the trap involves the rejection of her reality. Unable to recognize her own responses she simply relinquishes herself to trying to please Daddy. (p. 36)

For girls, who abandon their reality early, a later abandonment of self, in search of relatedness, easily follows. For me self-abandonment was not conscious, and manifested at times, in dissociation, naïve decisions and an unwillingness to see clues that could have afforded me some protection, clues that would later seem obvious. This description is not unusual for an ego blinded to natural feminine ground, an ego that is unable to trust the wisdom of intuitive intelligence, which can be a rich source of information that otherwise remains hidden in the unconscious field.

As my own initiation continues, my heart aches with worry over my husband, who during this period lost his job. (As you know, I would learn later, that this worry was unnecessary.) Not knowing that he is fine, I fight compulsions telling me to try to find him even though he is very consistent in communicating to me by phone, that family is a burden to him, that he does not love me or want me, nor is he willing to see his stepdaughter. He speaks in infrequent calls with cold, almost "mute" detachment.

I remember thinking to myself, "If he had a stroke, I would not leave his side. This is no different. He is having a breakdown." With this distorted ego position, I ignore psyche as she continues to attempt to lead me to the realization that my focus is sorely misplaced. This desire to play the saint, the faithful servant, is the detritus of my Catholic upbringing. So long ago, in a girlhood time, the suffering Mary, Mother of Jesus, enduring, standing by her man, the Pieta image was served up as a worthy model. This socio/spiritual value, though unconscious, undermines the connection with reality that I need in order to survive, muddling the swirling undercurrents of emotion that prevent me from finding solid ground.

Nonetheless, I am very slowly letting go of the unconscious fusion with my husband and the unhealthy sense that he is metaphorically my god. This strange confusion comes from an earlier belief that he would love and protect me and keep me safe and whole. With that belief, I project onto him the very Divine that resides within *my* center, my woman's being thereby giving myself away. This false and admittedly neurotic ideation begins crumbling, with the lumbering speed of a glacier, in the face of his cold disregard and what seems like an odd escape, much like an adolescent running away from home, into the Arizona desert.

While my woman's descent, through abandonment is devastating, redemption is experienced through a proportionately powerful encounter, or series of encounters, with a more real and feminine divine, who I also refer to as a Divine Other.

Not surprisingly, for a long time, even as redemption occurs, so too does descent. I am caught in a painfully recursive process that seems neither hierarchical nor linear. Words from Judy Grahn's (1987) stunning retelling of the Inanna myth come to mind in which Ereshkigal speaks in brutal honesty to Inanna. It is as if Ereshkigal is urging me to accept the reality of my difficult inner experience:

Can you bear your heart to be split
open and to lie so naked?

You will moan, Inanna
you will cry.

Everyone you ever were
will die,
while you go down.

We will
fight. Your heart will ooze like red meat.
I will suffer too, to birth you,
to transform and finally release you. (p. 55)

In the midst of this pain, I begin to experience an authentic Divine presence, who seemingly waits to be called. Transformation is forged when
one is in the swamplands, on one's knees, and calls out to a Divine, within
or without, for help. The Divine I pray to in the next part of this story is a
poiesis, an act of imagination, of image making, allowing me to access my
most sacred center of being, the Divine within.

For me, a woman who experiences, at this time of life, an inability to
trust, there is no belief that a Divine god would personally reach into my
world and respond to my cries. My experience of God had thus far been a
product of a patriarchal abstraction. To explain this loss of Divine connection, Meador's (1994) words are helpful:

> Women in our culture are separated from the pathways of their natural
> growth. Adapted to a religion of light and a culture that upholds light
> and reason, women are cut off from their roots and from their own
> creative transformative energies which lie in the chaos and mystery
> of the dark. (p116)

## REDEEMED BY THE EARTHBOUND GOD

What I need is an instinctual or earthbound theology. One grounded in
my woman's path, a theology honoring relationship, sensuality, intuitive
wisdom, and a Divine who lives in the dark recesses of my being.

Still, redemptive streams continue to flow as the Divine responds in
my internal and external world. By example, on one particular night, I had
been thrown into compulsions undergirded by feelings of loneliness and
terror, and in the midst of one such compulsion, cried out for grace and
guidance. I then experienced what was clearly an answer to my prayers.

This response came in the persons of unexpected visitors on a critical evening, as if the Divine willingly brought a literal gift of companionship to me as witness to her being.

I distinctly remember the evening, coming back from a late internship commitment. Without thinking or choosing, I made a sharp turn into a mini-mart. As if waking from a sleep, I realized I was going to get out of the car and get a bottle, or several bottles, of wine. In the moment of consciousness, I knew I planned to get drunk. Yet paradoxically, that was no plan of mine, not something I would do. I pulled out of the lot and started for home, without leaving my car.

Moments later, again I turned to go to the same store for the wine, for the purpose of getting drunk. Again I knew it wasn't I (my ego) who wanted this, but now I was afraid, even stunned, experiencing myself as almost powerless in the face of such an overwhelming compulsion.

I drove from the store, thankfully without having made a purchase, and moments later pulled off to the side of the road—to reflect and to try to stop the trembling that had overtaken me. I felt possessed and confused, yet I knew, at least intellectually, that underpinning and fuelling each compulsive act is something deep that threatens the ego.

I willed myself to stay in the moment, to perhaps feel, or even whiff the reality behind the compulsion. What could threaten me so that I would need to keep it in the unconscious? What could drive me, as a master drives a slave, toward the deeper haze of alcohol? It came to me, first in my body, like a muscle cramp that wakes one from sleep—one wakes, already in the throes of pain run amuck. Then I faced what came from the depths, the extent and horror of my aloneness, and then like a wave abandonment came that old presence, which is so dangerous to my soul. With that consciousness came grief and tears; my body gave itself to the sorrow, my head just lay on the steering wheel, and I cried, knowing the road I drove on had no lights, no shoulder, and that if I never made it home, no one would know or care. No one waited to greet me, no light was on, and there was no familiar ritual of tucking a child in or receiving a lover's caress. And not surprisingly, with consciousness and deep feeling came the release of the compulsion.

In this moment, the waters of descent ripped me from a solid rock wall of being, and in the many similar moments that followed, pulverized me—much as the waters of the Grand Canyon erode its walls to the fine sand that rests in the river's delta region, far below. This process is the soul's alchemical *solutio*, the washing away of that which is transformation through the dissolution of the waters.

This moment, in which all illusions—of myself as bright psychological intern, educational leader, able doctoral student—were crashed in the reality of my deeper identity, that of a profoundly lonely woman. Yet, embedded in that devastation was also the redemptive current.

In my story, I am on the side of the road; the tears and the heartache, for the moment, are spent. Out of an old, timeless place, redemption unfolds.

I say out loud, "Please help me. I am so alone. I cannot do this by myself." I am not really praying—I am too alone to pray, too alone to believe that the divine and I are friends. No, I am on my knees, so to speak, before empty space. There are no illusions now. Even in the absence of faith, a profound knowing enters me, and fills all of me with peace. That is all—and that is everything. I know nothing else, but peace. That is the great mystery, for the soul to cry out without even faith, and to experience a Divine response.

Feeling bone-tired, as if I am in the aftermath of a full-blown psychic seizure, I drive home. Thirty minutes later, at ten o'clock at night, after a 15-hour day of teaching and a psychotherapy internship, I approach my 10 acres and my unlit home. I notice—something unlikely and unusual—a pick-up truck in my driveway, barely visible in the moonlit night. The peace that had entered my being earlier signals complete calm.

It is then that I recognize Donna and Darrell, two sweet people who had begun cleaning my home 2 year before, though they did not work in that capacity now. As I approach the passenger side of the truck and look inside, I realize that Halloween cookies lay in Donna's lap. I know her words, before she speaks, "Darrell and I were driving home from Merced, and we thought you might like to have some cookies with us."

And so, in my friends this night, two faces of redemption are present, they are two angels, from the Greek word for messenger. Their presence in this particular moment is a clear communication, "You are not alone." Through them, the archetype, The Messenger, has manifested in the outer world.

They have responded to a whisper, "Go to Mary's home tonight. You do not need to be invited. You are sent. If she is not there, wait." One does not have to listen to such soulful callings, but in the grace of that profound encounter, they did.

As I look back, years later, I know that the Self also appeared to me, at that time, in dream images of wholeness and beauty. One such image was a large rising sun, which seemed to pulsate with peace and love, bringing

my waking body a feeling of transformative wholeness similar t
ported in some accounts of near-death experiences. This type
experience is, according to analyst Lionel Corbett (1996), one of ... ways
in which the numinous manifests as it performs its healing function.

For other abandoned women, the journey out of the darkness, the redemption, may be quite different. For me it was as if the Divine guided
me out, to the degree that I called to Her. The response was sometimes
literal and earthbound: sending friends to fix my washing machine, to hang
curtain rods, and on the night my dear friends Darrell and Donna came, to
share Halloween cookies when I was lost in loneliness. At other times, the
response was transcendent and deeply transforming. To one split off into
disembodied intellectual life, as I was, the earthbound gestures are much like
the experience of Marion Woodman (1985) in India, as she sat in her hotel
lobby literally dying from illness, a by-product of her descent. She writes:

> I sat on the end of a couch writing a letter. A large Indian woman in
> gold-trimmed sari squeezed between the side of the couch and me.
> Her fat arm was soft and warm. I pulled away to make room to write.
> She cuddled against me. I moved. She moved. (p. 179)

Woodman (1985) learned later that, upon seeing what he believed to be
an alone and dying woman, an Indian man had sent his wife to help her.

Her explanation of redemption as a move toward wholeness has very
deep cultural roots. She writes that, for women, wholeness has to do with
psychological pregnancy—the virgin forever a virgin, forever pregnant,
forever open to possibilities. It's important here to know that the early
Greek meaning for virgin, and Woodman's also, is a "free woman" with her
own integrity. The virgin was possessed by no man, rather she was earthy
and body affirming. For the Greeks, this wholeness of a woman was imagined as a butterfly. Like the butterfly, Woodman writes, a woman must
first emerge from a caterpillar and chrysalis.

Not everyone returns from underworld experiences. Some are irrevocably overwhelmed in this real and frightening place, as was Nietzsche;
some, like Jung, are buffeted about mercilessly and burdened to the brink
with the onslaught, yet return to achieve great acts of contribution. And
still others remain in a much less fortunate state in which a multitude of
life defenses allows them to disavow the reality of the realms between, in
which they are forever imprisoned.

## THE WOMAN IN THE WOODS

I wanted to be out of the darkness. My soul ached at times, but the work of transformation unfolded in its own time. What brought me hope was an understanding of the soulful woman I was becoming. I first imagined this transformed inner personality in a wooded circle beside a night fire. It was at a time when I needed help in making a most difficult decision. (It is the inner woman, not the details of the dilemma, that matters here.)

This inner woman, as I imagined her, was graceful, her hair long, elegant, and white, standing shoeless at last, toes embracing the earth, symbolic of the earthbound instinctual self. This "becoming" woman was less judgmental than I. She had forgiven wrongs against her; she intuitively knew the pain and joy embedded in the decision at hand, yet she communicated to me with equanimity, that I should move forward anyway.

This inner woman, whose image came through active imagination rather than through a dream, was present as I imagined a willing release of my husband to a Divine Other, which freed me to experience the continuing work of Ereshkigal. Now I experience a new relationship with the Divine as Self, characterized by inner wholeness, trust, and feminine instinctual life. It was after I began consciously to know this woman that I realized that I was closer to redemption than to descent. I believe that I could not have experienced her in the imaginal field if her embodiment in my conscious life was not close at hand.

## THE EVISCERATING MOUNTAIN LION

In this story, you have seen psyche and I, journeying together from the beginning days of descent. Our route resembled those of accomplished pilots, moving, for instance, from New York City to Las Angeles. When seen from a distance, those routes move in a steady journey line. And yet we know that the skilled pilots shift and change their courses throughout, knowing this is the way to navigate unseen, powerful air currents and a host of weather conditions. This was the way of psyche, her imaginal figures, and me, often shifting yet moving ahead. Psyche delivered one last essential dream, whose image would crack wide open the last rigid ego attitude preventing me from completing my work. With this one dream, the ego's hold on me was shattered like fine glass, unable to withstand the clarity of an image whose

true vibrating note would not be denied. This final dream image, of an unlikely couple, set me irrevocably, powerfully, joyfully free.

### The Mountain Lion Dream

I am in my home, once shared by my husband, our daughter, and me,
the home in which I now live, alone. Its cathedral ceilings and large
bank of windows allow light to flood the cavernous living room. I am
aware that there is no furniture anywhere, nowhere to eat, no utensils
with which to prepare food. I see a beautiful staircase separating the
bedrooms above from the 1st floor. At its base, on a section of floor
that is covered with cold hard tile, a mountain lion and I are coupling.
(Harrell, Dream Journal, 2000)

Upon waking, I had the idea that this was a positive dream. In Jungian psychology there is the idea of a *coniunctio*. In Samuels, Shorter and
Plaut's (1996) *Critical Dictionary of Jungian Analysis,* a *coniunctio* is an alchemical symbol of a union deep within the psyche that results in the
birth of a new element, perhaps, a new attitude. When coniunctio symbols "…(i.e. man and woman, king and queen, Sol and Luna, cock and
hen)" (p. 35) appear, they may symbolize a positive or negative occur-
rence within the psyche. The outcome, we know from Jung, depends on
the attitude of the conscious mind. I wondered, did this dream symbolize the renewal of an ego position? If it did, I was utterly clueless about
the nature of this position.

For what happened next, as I shared the dream in my therapy session, I
will be forever grateful. Skillfully and with careful analysis my Jungian-oriented psychotherapist, Dr. T., asked three, *only three*, elegant questions.
His questions and my honest answers changed everything, dealing a final
blow to an irascible ego attitude, which had forced me into an unhealthy
collusion with my abandonment situation. Here's how the questions and
answers proceeded:

Dr. T.:   Did you enjoy the sex with the mountain lion?

Mary:   No. I didn't like it at all. (With this answer, to a question I hadn't
          considered before, the *coniunctio*-related smile left my face.)

Dr. T.:   Then why didn't you stop it?

Mary:   I couldn't, because I was terrified. Did you ever see a moun-
          tain lion? With one powerful swoop of his clawed paw he could

eviscerate me, decapitate me, break my neck. I couldn't risk it. (I was shocked at this idea, that I feared being harmed by the mountain lion. I didn't recall that feeling of fear in the dream.)

Dr. T.:  Who is f ***ing you, while you are too afraid to stop it?

Mary:  My husband. Then I hear what I have said, "My husband!"

I was not claiming a literal act, but stating my heretofore unconscious opinion of what was going on between my husband and me, what I was allowing.

I feared that I would not be safe, feared his cold, silent aggression, and feared that the harsh way, in which I had seen him treat others, would be turned on me. Though it is true, that in those dark days I had been frightened of so much, I had not known that I feared him. Now I could admit out loud, and to myself, my true emotional reality: if I asserted myself in any way I risked the retaliation of a man who liked to describe himself as, "The iron fist in the velvet glove." This truth rushed into consciousness where it remained, honest and open. The fiction that I was a woman who loved, but did not fear, her husband was exposed, and a new ego attitude emerged. Surprisingly, once my fear was acknowledged and felt by me, it lost its potency. I experienced a new strength in owning my reality.

Within days, I called him on the phone, still not knowing where in the desert he lived, and told him that I would seek a divorce, that I would seek it now, and that the court proceedings would take place in California, where I lived. I was not afraid. I was angry, calm, and clear. And so it happened.

Fifteen years have passed since that period of descent. The woman I have become often surprises me. When I catch myself in the emotions or actions of this new way of being, it is like catching myself in the mirror after a big physical change like a weight loss or gain, or pregnancy, or after I cut my long hair, then forget that it is gone. At first I say, "Who is that?" Then quickly I remember, "It's I. This is who I am."

What I catch in the soulscape's mirror is the sound of my own frequent laughter. It is spontaneous and rich and comes from the most authentic part of me. Or I'll find myself singing show tunes, or I'll hear the college students partying in a rental on my block and rather than be annoyed or feel invaded by their world, I will feel glad to be near their youth and community. Even as a university professor, I am surprised that they invite me to their parties and more surprised that I sometimes go and am able to partake of them in this way. I am here also in the moment of writing my lived life, bringing meaning from my woman's journey to the world.

In all of these moments of recognition of the woman I have become, I am reminded of a moving term in Goodchild (2001), "creation's longing" (p. 63). Creation longs for us to embrace her, longs for us to live our fate. And when we create a more trustworthy relationship with our embodied being, and the Self within, creation celebrates.

*** *** ***

## THE DIVINE OTHER

The Divine Other in the story is often presented (by me) as if She exists "out there" or "up there," as if The Divine is an entity other than the most sacred part of the self within. The idea of the Divine Other in my story is indeed an essential part of psychological wholeness. Let me explain. As I have said, to pray to God in the context of my story is an act of poiesis, an act of image making, for my soul must create an image of the recipient of the prayer. This Divine to which I call is hidden behind the god image, hidden because the Divine is a mystery. The Divine is not a fiction, but rather a very real imaginal figure with intentionality and autonomy. I pray through the lens of a poetic image, which has me on my knees, and in this gesture, She to whom I pray is in the heavens.

In this act of imagination, the reality is the Divine Other. The image that allows me to "see through" to Her essence is what is created by soul. Whether referencing a Higher Power, The Source, The Great Mother, God the Father, the Divine Within, Sophia, or the Self, from my depth psychological perspective, I am addressing The Divine center of being.

In myth, the golden ring or the tiny doll, as in the Russian folktale titled, The Baba Yaga, are examples of symbols of this Divine element. In myth and in literal life the Divine impulse might constellate whenever unconscious, or conscious content threatens to overwhelm the ego in a difficult situation. When the Divine enters, it is as if a grace presents itself, emanating from a deep and sacred center within, allowing the person in distress to navigate an otherwise impossible task.

I see this in my psychotherapy practice, for instance, when an individual is trying to work through the unacceptable death of a child. The task quickly reaches a point in which the parent hits a wall of steel in the mourning process: grief and longing become overwhelming and a future without the beloved seems annihilating. This too is a disorienting descent in which individuals have neither adequate preparation, nor compensatory systems in place to aid them in navigating such a loss. At such times, the infusion of the Divine allows a forward movement of the mourning task.

## FORGING A CANYON: EROSIVE WATERS OF SOUL

In drawing the following comparison between the archetype of descent and that very physical natural dynamic that created the exquisite Grand Canyon, I experience an eco-cosmological transference to my topic. By the term eco-cosmological transference, I mean that it is as if the natural world becomes ensouled and places something of her deep self into the archetypal process that I am describing, just as I project a measure of my own experience into the natural world. In other words, the natural world and I are not completely separate from each other. For me, descent is like the creative forging of the Grand Canyon. Just as the waters of the Colorado River literally tore away the canyon rock, transforming the land, the descent process carved away who I had been. After almost pulverizing my ego and my soul, descent rendered something much better.

The Grand Canyon is undergirded and surrounded by massive formations of rock, and yet the erosive waters cut through that rock, over time. Through the ages, her hunger relentlessly devours all that stands in the way of her creative process. For me, this unremitting transformation is an image of the soulful journey of descent. It is a process by which the natural chthonic feminine, imaged by the snake and the tornado, is fully alive, just as she is alive in the creation of canyon walls.

For me, the rock walls of the canyon hold the symbology of ego realities. The ego, like the rock, experiences itself as all that there is, impenetrable and larger than the great cosmology of which it is a small part. Yet ego consciousness, in the end, is nothing in the dissolution of the waters.

From the distance of time and space, one can easily see the beauty of the rock strata, those high walls left by the water's movement, and marvel at the eons of transformation each layer claims. After the transformative work is done, one is awed at the glorious meanders of the river, the abundant wildlife that dwells in its rock banks, and doesn't care, really, for the moments in which the river cut the rock, boulder by boulder, and ground the very earth herself to fine sand.

Because I am possessed of ego consciousness, I, unlike the rock, do remember the many moments in which the waters of the descent tore down my ego walls, piece by piece. My dream images recounted in those days the dissolution of who I was—the glass high-rise careening to the ground, the cutoff yellow rose, and the abandoned 13-year-old girl child.

One such event was mentioned in the memoir above, when the illusions of who I thought myself to be were torn apart as I faced my loneliness on the side of the country road. It is a moment, in its particularity, in which the waters of descent did tear down a section of ego, reforming it, making it more real, connecting ego with soul.

The rock wall of the Grand Canyon, like the ego, is transformed into something much finer. When it is no longer rock, when it is small smooth pebbles or fine sand, low in the river's delta region, the rock-turned-sand has lived out its fate. It belongs to something profound; it is neither the canyon, the river, nor the rock from which it was ground, and yet, it is all of these. It rests at the place where it was meant finally to be. It has lived out its destiny.

It is a particular quality of human ego consciousness, which designates the canyon grand, its walls majestic, its waters magnificent, and the sand at the bottom, poor. To the cosmos and to me, the fine sand is beautifully diverse in weight, density, and color; its purpose and being as grand as all the rest. If it is difficult for humankind to grasp the significance of the transformed sand, how much more difficult is it to know the wonder of a transformed soul. That is why archetypes of transformation are considered to be mysteries, to all, that is, but soul's longing. She always knows that transformation is what one's soul must achieve. Soul longs for the living out of one's fate and does not fear the pain of transformation. Although I am a different woman now, I wish to end with a journal entry in which I first became conscious of this new way of being:

Every once-in-awhile when I least expect it, I notice a peace and contentment within. I am aware that there is no anxiety, no deep longing, no feeling of dis-ease, and no fantasizing about the return of a husband who I never really knew until his leaving redeemed me. I am with myself in the moment and that is enough. This sense of wholeness rests with me, as a delicate butterfly momentarily visits a flower. These moments are entirely new to me. They hold a profound quality and feel like a reconnecting with a precious part of myself. (Harrell, Personal Journal, 2002)

# STORIES FROM THE SHADOWLANDS

The stories in this chapter share a recurring theme, the archetypal shadow. By briefly reflecting on the definition of shadow, I aim to provide my reader with clarity and context so that she or he might wonder with me, and come along more comfortably as we enter the imaginal realm within each story.

Jung (1994/1954) explains shadow as those psychological parts of personality that have been repressed or forgotten. For a simple illustration of shadow, imagine a family album. Notice the pictures celebrating birthdays, graduations, the day the new puppy arrived, weddings, and so on. Where's the photo showing the day father came home drunk, or the moment the family discovered that sister Joan was addicted to heroin, or the night brother Ennis punched a hole in his bedroom wall? Not in the album? Indeed. These are the "stuff" of family shadow—powerful, existing, yet relegated to the basement of experience.

Like all shadow content, when and if those troublesome family events reach the light of awareness, issues can be resolved, treatments found, and outside forces brought to bear. When not disowned or repressed, problematic shadow material often brings individuals, families, and cultures opportunities to realize their full potential, to realize rich capacities of being.

To illustrate this idea of realized potential and capacities of being, imagine a family culture in which a mother's drinking is kept in the shadows. No one speaks of it. Each family member protects the mother from the consequences of her drinking. Instead of openly speaking of her constant drunken state, children and relatives create fictions. "Mom likes to party," or "Mom's not feeling well today."

Additionally, no one in the system allows herself to experience authentic feelings related to mom's drunken behavior. Anger, grief over loss of nurturing, and much more, live in a repressed and voiceless domain. These broader family realities, as well as mom's disease, are relegated to the shadowlands of experience. By contrast, picture the mother who enters a detox facility, fully embraces rehabilitation, enters an aftercare program, and—admitting that she is an alcoholic—begins a lifetime of AA meetings through which she reclaims her life. The children have a mother; she may be late in returning to her motherhood but she is fully present. The family begins to heal, learning to speak their truth, learning to laugh, to cry, to express and embrace life together, a functional family in recovery. This family, as well as the mother, is claiming its potential.

One aim of psychotherapy is the resolution of difficulties (disease) generated by the unconscious presence of shadow. Jung instructs psychologists to:

> ...observe the sporadic emergence, whether in the form of images or feelings, of those dim representations, which detach themselves in the darkness from the invisible realm of the unconscious and move as shadows before the interned gaze. In this way things repressed and forgotten come back again. This is a gain in itself, though often a painful one, for the inferior and even the worthless belongs to me as my shadow and gives me substance and mass. (p. 59)

Jung's claim that shadow material can give us "substance and mass" is seen in the family story above. When the alcoholism of the mother moved through her leadership from family shadow to conscious content, the family could then begin a process of becoming substantive and solid, no longer wobbling Jell-O-like through a labyrinth of confusion and half-truths.

Additionally, when speaking of shadow material, we often use the term *dark*, referring specifically to that which is unconscious, often thought by the ego to be unseemly, diminished, or too problematic to accept. Shadow figures appear in the dreams of all individuals, in some cases presenting attitudes that are closer to consciousness and therefore easier to interpret. This type of shadow problem is more manageable.

To underscore the essential point, the immediate goal of the study of the unconscious is to reach a state in which the unconscious contents no longer remain unconscious, but are in relationship with the conscious ego. What Jung (1953/1977) said of the complexes is true of shadow aspects of individual and cultural personality: So long as they are unconscious, they are "disturbing factors that break through the unconscious control and act like true 'disturbers of the peace'" (p. 232).

## PROLOGUE TO A NATION DREAMS ITS VIOLENCE

The first story, "A Nation Dreams Its Violence" is not so much a story as a dream, a national dream, and its central shadow figure being a low fellow who goes by the name of national violence. Unfortunately, this cultural imaginal figure, like all shadow figures, continues to remain in the societal unconscious, its impulses leaking out, bringing chaos and death to innocents on an almost biweekly basis. As school shootings and mass killings at malls, theaters, and government installations proliferate in the United States, confusion grows to the degree that the "shooters'" motives are considered and overanalyzed while the mover and shaker of the phenomenon, national violence, goes largely unnoticed, existing only as a quasi-curiosity.

Notice that I am drawing a distinction between individuals' violent actions and societal attitudes. Each plays a different role in the series of mass shootings and specifically, school shootings. The individual actors take center stage in the country's consciousness (national ego), while the unconscious societal attitude of national violence remains disowned, unexamined, experienced as innocent and sadly, deeply embedded.

I tell this particular dream story to shine a heightened quality of light on this archetypal presence. It is clear to me that until unexamined national violence is unmasked, the repetition of senseless killings will continue in America. Simply put, the shadow archetype of national violence seeks out compromised individuals (the mentally ill or young men on the sometimes confusing cusp of manhood) and moves through them much like engorged waters seek the weak points of an old dam from which to escape, first in slow trickles, then violent torrents, an idea that I will revisit below.

In this dreamscape, I call attention to specific, literal events—a series of school shootings occurring over time and on a national level—and simultaneously interpret and seek meaning. As I personally witness these events, I initially experience myself as a waking person observing through the media a cultural dream. While not usually present in the geographic location of each event, the exact point measured by longitude and latitude, I and we feel a constriction deep within, a sad and helpless resonance with each life lost, or each family forever changed. And so, each of us is a participant in an in-between, subtle, and tragic world.

In the last segment of this story, I'll examine, as I have with previous stories, personal affects and beliefs that may have shaped my own experience and describe the interactive field in which the shadow manifests. In "A Nation Dreams Its Violence" I offer a new picture for society's photo album, a cultural attitude that supports streams of violence in movies, in quiet and private hate talk, in ignoring (then blaming) the marginalized and the socially violated, and finally in isolating the emotionally compromised.

I offer one final caution: while you may see clear images of *individuals* engaged in violence, this will not be so for the chief object of our interest, national violence. As we know, shadow is not clearly defined or easily identified. Therefore, as we enter the national dreamscape, we will be given symbols, the dream images that point to the culprit. We learned from Jung that a symbol is not the thing itself, but only points to the thing. To help us understand this, he tells us that the symbol is not the moon but only the finger pointing to the moon. And so we carefully wonder about both literal realities and symbolism pointing to a deeper meaning.

## A NATION DREAMS ITS VIOLENCE

### PADLOCKS AND SENTRIES

Between 1996 and 2000, eight major school shootings turned a nation on its head. Nine boy shooters killed two teachers, 30 young people were killed, 72 students were wounded, and three parents were killed, all in schools thought to be safe.

What we know in 2015 is that the escalation of school shootings in American schools since April 20, 1999, the year of the Columbine High School tragedy, has been staggering. For instance, on December 2012, in Newtown, Connecticut 26, 1st graders and educators were killed, shot by 20-year-old Adam Lanza. What many do not know, however, is that between that tragic day in Newtown and 12 months later, there were 14 more school shootings (retrieved from Wikipedia on September 13, 2013). If the current escalation in school shootings continues at its present rate, the United States will see close to a 300% rise in school shootings between 2010 and 2020.

I am compelled to share the following analysis in which I look imaginally at what is occurring. I especially focus on images from Columbine High School, in Colorado, on April 20, 1999 and Pearl High School, in Pearl, Mississippi, on October 1, 1997, not because these events were any more or less troubling than others, but because they may hold answers that will inform all these tragic events.

Before becoming a psychologist, I completed many years as a classroom teacher at the kindergarten to 12th (K-12) level and later, as a college professor. As I go back in time, I remember the following experience, and quickly move to a nontemporal, present moment of soul. Here's what occurs as I move into this fluid and deep space.

I see, as if simultaneously, hundreds of faces in all the student-filled schoolyards and college campuses I've walked through. I know these faces; they belong to my students. The school in which I teach on April 20, 1999 is in California. Yet somehow the bullets fired by young boys on K-12 campuses, even before the April 20th tragedy, (in Springfield, Illinois; West Paducah, Kentucky; Pearl, Mississippi; and Jonesboro, Arkansas), have found their way to the soul of my campus.

For many, like me, the knowing is painfully conscious, for others this gnosis lives only in what Robert Sardello (1999) calls a "constriction of soul," a place without conscious image where fear lives in the body's altered breathing, forgetfulness, or anxious watchfulness. As a school community, we, like many others, keep the side entrances to our rural school grounds locked throughout the day. Teachers and parents fight unwieldy padlocks as we exit the grounds for lunch or to meet obligations within the school district. I remember that in my early days of teaching, the padlocks that secured the campuses were never used during the school daylight hours, but only at night and on weekends to protect the schools against minor vandalism. As I think of this change, a quiet sadness emerges, like flotsam from a lost ship, its wreckage lazily bumping into itself.

In 1999, most schools secure all except the main entrance where a trusted sentry on duty checks visitors in and out. Such "practical" and seemingly straightforward actions on behalf of the children's safety gnaw at consciousness, whispering that a culture's fragmentation is much closer than the distance between our California community and West Paducka, Springfield, or any other site of a school tragedy.

We learn on this April day that two students at Columbine High School in Littleton, Colorado entered their school building and cruelly, mercilessly, massacred 12 fellow students and one teacher, then took their own lives. Long after that shooting, I continue to be haunted by both the young gunmen and the victims.

It is this haunting many years later that demands voice. For me, all the early musings and too-simple answers by the media, experts, and perplexed onlookers have not adequately addressed the central recurring question: Why is this happening to our children and what does this phenomenon say about the national culture? To answer these questions, I find myself pondering the shootings as a postmodern cultural dream and seeking meaning in the dream's imaginal figures.

Archetypal scholars assert that all cultural bodies, including nations, experience unconscious activities such as dreaming. One groundbreaking book titled *Technology as Symptom and Dream* (Romanyshyn, 1992) provides a thorough and clear example of how these scholars work through and analyze cultural content. We know that dreams are purposeful actions of psyche whose aim is cultural individuation (Tarnas, 1991), the ultimate movement toward wholeness. If the concretized school shootings are her dream images, then psyche wants us to enter her dreamer's soul, for the purpose of making meaning, and to experience the underside, the shadow, of cultural imagination.

Dreams are not rational, even while they are meaningful. Therefore, as I enter the world of school shootings as one enters a dream, it may feel like a story that doesn't seem linear or sensible. I suggest that you simply agree to wonder, to stay for a while in waters of unknowing. That's what we all do when we enter a personal dream. Therefore, that is what we must do when we enter a national dreamscape.

## ENTERING THE DREAM: FIRST OBSERVATIONS

Certainly the dream of shootings in American schools, which is both imaginal and tragically literal, lives in a chaotic landscape of soul. My first observation as I begin to unravel meaning is that the lost lives of young people are concrete images, a particularly troubling observation from a perspective of dream interpretation. Just as psychotic individuals experience a blurred line between the symbolic and concrete, so too does this dreaming nation.

When the dreamer can't tell the difference between the symbol and the concrete, there is a probability of a psychosis. And so, I wonder, are we facing a dynamic of an America out of touch with its own reality?

As I comment on a 2nd observation, that we are face to face with an archetypal experience, I offer a reminder for readers new to Jungian thought: an archetype is defined by Jung (1953/1977) as a pattern of human experience. One identifies the archetypal qualities of image by sensing that the image being considered is linked to and part of other related, repetitive, and deeper images. Often in archetypal dreams, the images are more difficult to understand, often pointing to something larger than the personal and therefore, leaving us at a loss for associations. All of the markers that point to the presence of an archetype are surely in this dream. It would seem undeniable that violence regarding this series of school shootings is a frightening pattern of human experience. We observe that in every part of our beings, each shocking report of yet another school shooting links immediately, and on multiple levels, to the shootings that came before and ominously to the ones that we fear will follow. All of the images we hear about, read about, and worry about are most difficult to understand and most of us cannot articulate personal associations ("This shooting reminds me of when I..."). So far, all of this sounds worrisome so you may be wondering why we would want to look at this aspect of national life. You may ask, "If all of this is repressed from consciousness, then why don't we just let it be?"

My answer is a simple answer of hope. Within the dream images of our western, patriarchal culture is a promise that a willingness to host the image may result in a de-escalation of destructive dream action. Most importantly, hosting the image may well save national psyche from continuing to live out its disowned violence in fate, a fate currently enacted in our schools.

So what are we to do? Hillman (1983b) writes that to host an image is to dialogue with it, to be informed by it, a process much like the ancient custom of paying homage to the gods. It is through this hosting that the ego is relativized, where the conscious self is brought into balance with its unconscious. From the perspective of the imaginal, it is necessary for societal consciousness to revisit the images of the school shootings in a soulful, and therefore, transformative way.

As we begin to look more deeply, we start with a central dream figure, the guns, a topic with which societal consciousness is most familiar. As we begin deepening our understanding of this image, much more emerges.

## SOUL CANNOT DIGEST METAL

In the dream of school shootings, I see a dreamscape inhabited by violent shadow characters wielding metallic weapons, including a powerful .30-.30 caliber rifle, a .22-caliber Ruger pistol and a .22-caliber semiautomatic rifle. As I "host" the particular image of the weapons, I ask myself, what do I need to remember? What associations do I have to these objects? Why did psyche bring these particular images to the dream? Then I begin to remember that in dream analysis, the presence in dreams of hard, cold metal objects suggests that an attitude or situation is present which soul cannot digest. In the collective experience of the nation's past 200 plus years, the image of metal weaponry is a constant. In the national shootings as dream series, the guns are collective figures associated with death and violence, not with a dignified protection of hearth and home as echoed in the United States Constitution's guarantee of its populace's "right to bear arms," so often quoted by gun advocates. In this cultural dream on the issue of guns, the unconscious attitude is in sharp contrast to the conscious attitude. We might wonder, "Is Psyche, who always sends dreams for the dreamer's benefit, hoping we will see the conflict and adjust the conscious attitude?"

As we continue considering the weapons as dream images, let us also note that the weaponry seems to be driven by archetypal energies as much as by the persons of the boy shooters. Additionally, there is a rigid and cold, yet twisted quality to this image of guns held by boys shooting peers and teachers, and also murdering parents in preschool hours. I notice too that even as they kill, these boys are not otherwise socially engaged, acting within a lifeless frame of emotional distance, mirroring a lifeless inner world.

In the dreamscape, we notice that the use of the weapons, and certainly the result of their use is grotesque, twisted much like that of Picasso's famous painting, titled Guernica. Picasso was one of the first modern artists who painted soul reality by distorting and at times, perverting the literal in order to reveal the real (Jaffe, 1983), just as our dream does. In this now famous Guernica painting, you may remember that Picasso gave the viewer images of women, children, men, and animals in foul suffering, depicting the village of Guernica in northern Spain as it was bombed in 1937 during the Spanish Civil War.

I remember as a young girl decades ago, coming upon this painting in a very large room, in what I believe was in New York's Metropolitan

Museum of Art. The only other item in the room was a lone bench. I will never forget sitting on that bench for hours unable to look away, just as I cannot look away from this dream now.

It was only Picasso's distortions and misshapen forms that could depict the reality of war (a reality that was necessary to communicate to others in a pretelevision era what was occurring). This same collective unconscious that creates the art creates the dream, all in the service of national soul. In dreams as in art, psyche is offering us transformative insight: just as soul could not digest bombs falling on the village of Guernica, it cannot digest metal weapons, especially when they are aimed at our children. The presence of the guns in the national dream says to me that as the cultural impulse toward violence is owned, it can be successfully inhibited, contained, or transformed, ideas that are explored below.

## THE FIGURES OF THE BOYS

As an observing dreaming ego, I ask, "Why are almost all of the school shooters boys?" The culture often personifies its nation as feminine. So for the sake of imaginal analysis and to offer answers, I will consider our nation as a dreaming archetypal feminine figure. Thus, I suggest that this is her (the nation's) dream. In dream theory, when a woman's psyche presents male figures, these represent her contrasexual part of personality, her animus, that part of self, developed or not, representing the rational, the forward moving, and also embodying the power principal.

Male symbols imagined in this dream as white boys who kill, bear little resemblance to the societal, positive attitude that holds its white male citizens to be civilized, productive, and to a large degree, law abiding. (This attitude is supported by the disproportionately large numbers of black young men incarcerated in this country.) The dream shooters are neither rational, nor forward moving in their lives; any claim to power would only relate to destruction or the negative power principle.

These boy images in such violent, hateful, and rage-filled dream action are presenting a demanding question, "What cultural adjustments are necessary?" I continue my search for an answer by asking yet another question, "Is it significant that all the perpetrators are in beginning or late stages of puberty, one of several critical life positions that invite visitation by archetypal, and sometimes psychologically destabilizing energies?" I notice too that these boys live within a milieu in which no meaningful puberty rites accompany important life transitions. They are often separated from, or unable to access respectful, engaged, and meaningful relationships with men, whom we might think of as tribal elders. Thus, each boy in this dreamscape is left alone to contain his confusion, fear, and pain.

Though some current research suggests that adolescence is not the confusing, volatile time previously cited in the literature, I disagree, reminding the reader that we are talking of the unconscious position of these males, not necessarily their ego (conscious) experience. The dream action insists on the presence of explosive emotional unrest.

In the histories of many cultures, boys were initiated from one stage of life to another by tribal customs characterized by entering life and death situations, enduring pain and scarring, and exercising immeasurable courage. In these rituals, usually performed in sacred and secluded spaces, they were accompanied and contained by elder males.

One example of an ancient rite of manhood continues today in Papua New Guinea (Published Dec 26, 2011, You Tube, National Geographic). Initiates ranging in ages from 11 to 30 years old voluntarily gather in a hut they call the spirit hut. Until this ritual is completed, they will not be considered men, nor can they take their place as leaders.

For six weeks they are deeply cut by tribal experts in body patterns resembling that which crocodiles bear. To make sure each scar finds its most extreme protrusion, the initiates, after the painful cutting, wash daily in nearby waters. They are tended throughout by caring uncles, who know that no matter what suffering or challenges life brings these initiates, each will remember that they traversed this painful journey to manhood. The uncles hold the knowledge that afterwards all of life's suffering is easily contained by the memories of their courage in the earlier initiatory experience. When the young men return to the village, bodies bearing proud alligator-like scarring, they are greeted with unbridled joy and tribal celebration.

In the absence of effective modern cultural rites, we might consider that our nation's young men, lacking psycho-spiritual containment, are poorly served. Though some manage the transition well enough, others sadly do not. I am not suggesting that our young men should suffer in the Papua New Guinea manner, but that they do need cultural initiations, including deep relationships with wise elders who walk with them and help them contain their pain, and witness the depth of their courage as they move through the transitional journey. A good example of elders standing with initiates of all ages as they transform are the "old timers" in AA's 12-step program. They teach, they support, and they hold in awareness the path to a life of dignity. These elders walk with the initiates so that they can reenter the tribe in joy and celebration.

Could Columbine's Eric Harris and Dylan Klebold have been caught in a culture that failed to contain and support them, and also failed to provide inhibitions toward negative impulses? Could archetypal violence have entered them and possessed them at a precarious developmental stage? Is it possible that while they chose to be destructive (and therefore responsible), they were also impelled by unmanageable affect, and overwhelmed by destructive impulses? From an analytical psychological lens (a Jungian lens), possession is the overwhelming of the ego by the unconscious (Culbert-Koehn, 1998). We might be wise to consider that a current possession, both at an individual and a cultural level, is imaged in this national dream and embodied in the boy shooters.

How can our nation's boys effectively manage hate and rage when they live in a society that splits all aspects of the human condition into good and evil? I agree with Whitmont (2001), who writes that the current Western cultural theophany splits good and bad, light and dark, calling that which is dark, evil, banishing it from the human condition. With such splitting, instinctive needs such as aggression, hate, or greed will erupt in destruction. It bears repeating that when human instinct is denied, it cannot be inhibited or transformed. Can this splitting inform us on other issues, bullying for instance? On one side of the split, a child is told by his bully, "You are other, not fit to exist; you are not me." On the other side of the split, the victim might say, "I am bullied by you; therefore, I hate you. You don't deserve to live." Both positions are extreme splits distorting what is true.

Edinger's remarks echo this caution against splitting human capacities into good and evil. He wisely tells us that the Judeo-Christian cultural stance, as old as the patriarchal worldview, is to deny the shadow aspect of the human condition, to split it from itself and personify it as "the devil," thus ensuring unconscious eruption (unknown date, audiotape, Remarks on Answer to Job, C. G. Jung Los Angeles Institute Lectures). When we see a devil "out there" we will eventually project him onto another being; it is too easy to see the other as an "evil-doer" to use an unfortunate term from the Afghanistan and Iraqi wars, referring to the Taliban, al Qaeda, and later to all extremists. Under this reduction of a human to "other," it is then easier to kill him. What we are asked to do in depth psychology is to first discover, then transform the negative or destructive impulse within our own being. I have heard the idea put this way, "My analysis is not complete until I find the Hitler within." This ownership is not literally saying, "I am Hitler." Rather, it is recognition that each of us has Hitler-like capacities within and knowing that can choose not to live out of that destructive state. This is a process much different from denial, or splitting. It is taking responsibility for deciding which seeds within will be watered and which will not.

The dream series of school shooters brings us particular boys, some of whom are described by words such as loner, quiet, or nice, often with ego states not strong enough to defend against the powers of archetypal eruption. Fragments of the young killers' concrete worlds float in and out of awareness, just as the dream images do. When he was a 16 year old, Luke Woodman on October 1, 1997 shot two students and the assistant bandleader at Pearl High School in Mississippi, and wounded seven others. Though earlier on that day he fatally bludgeoned and stabbed his mother, he claimed that he couldn't remember it (Cloud, 1999).

I wonder at Luke Woodman's fascination with the alienation of Friedrich Nietzsche. A growing number of young people, both in an out of the mainstream, share a bond with this existential thinker. Woodman's fate, in which alienation and uncontained rage dominated, is a Dionysus' experience. You may remember this god of unbridled excess and madness by his Roman name, Bacchus. Though his more popular image is one of limitless celebration, we want to remember that he, like all archetypal personifications, has both positive and negative aspects. The following note Woodman gave a school peer shortly before he began shooting clearly demonstrates unbridled rage and alienation:

> I am not insane, I am angry. I killed because people like me are mistreated every day. I did this to show society, push us and we will push back. …All throughout my life, I was ridiculed, always beaten, always hated. Can you, society, truly blame me for what I do? Yes, you will. …It was not a cry for attention, it was not a cry for help. It was a scream in sheer agony saying that if you can't pry your eyes open, if I can't do it through pacifism, if I can't show you through the displaying of intelligence, then I will do it with a bullet. (Retrieved from Wikipedia on March 14, 2014)

A particular insight shared by archetypalist Richard Tarnas (1991) links Woodman's identification with Nietzsche to the events of October 1, 1997, when he wrote that each epochal transformation in the history of the West was "initiated by a kind of archetypal sacrifice" (p. 395). Socrates was a martyred prophet of Classical Greeks, Jesus of Christianity, and Galileo of modern science. He then argues that Friedrich Nietzsche may very well emerge as the prophet of the postmodern era.

The dream characters require that we adults of the culture must hold this connection in conscious awareness, a connection between archetypal phenomena and what seems at first glance, to be a marginalized pop cultural hero. Our children who identify with Nietzsche are telling us that they may also be one with excessive isolation, madness, internal imprisonment, and potentially, human sacrifice.

It seems important to note that parents of young men would be helped immensely, if we in the mental health field sound louder, more insistent warning bells when children begin to isolate for long periods of time. In his first interview since Newtown, Adam Lanza's father (Solomon, 2014) described what was to me Adam's frightening pattern of escalating, years-long isolation from his father, his brother Ryan, and later his mother— whom he shot four times before leaving for school on that fateful day in Newtown, Connecticut. As with other perpetrators of school violence, Adam suffered from a mental illness, a pervasive cognitive deficit. For him it was Asperger's syndrome (now subsumed under autism spectrum disorder). This means he would likely have difficulty understanding what emotions are, and how to read the emotional signals of others. Having Asperger's does *not* mean that he would have a lack of concern about hurting others, a marker for psychopathy. Yet in his isolation, Adam developed an online obsession with mass murders. A deadly (and previously undiagnosed) psychopathy emerged. What resulted was the sacrifice of 20 children, 7 adults—counting Adam's mother—and Adam himself.

The term "human sacrifice" may sound overstated, yet one needs only to look at our dead children, and adults, as well as the shooters, 50% of whom also die (Solomon, 2014), to know that this is an apt description. If we understand this phenomenon of human bloodshed and sacrifice then, perhaps we educators in the schools can stop tolerating the irrelevant in our work with students and move to the more real. To understand what part school cultures may play in all of this, we need to take a look at the Goddess archetype, one aspect of the feminine.

## THE RETURN OF THE GODDESS

You may have noticed that in analytical psychology much is made of myth. This is because all myth holds projections of the human experience. Myth, as all good literature, is the story psyche (the unconscious) tells about what humans feel or need; it also speaks of tragedy, pathos, loss, and transformation. If we look carefully at the myth traditions, we gain a valuable insight. So when we speak of this god or that, as I will soon speak of the Great Goddess, we are simply reflecting the great mystery capacities within all of us. The Goddess, like all archetypal aspects, lives within both men and women, as well as in cultures. Sometimes she manifests; sometimes she lives in shadow.

It is the myth of Dionysus, the consort of the Great Goddess in matriarchal theology, which allows us to see the psychological dynamic of young men, like Luke Woodman, resorting to excessive violence. In the myth, Dionysus always accompanies the Great Goddess (Whitmont, 2001); his wild and escalating sexual experience becomes destructive. Dionysus (symbol of all excess, including rage, greed, violence, etc.) is in the end torn apart and devoured by the Great Goddess. It may surprise you to know that if you studied this myth deeply you would discover not a literal devouring, but the symbology of divine transformation and containment, the two central processes unavailable to the boys in our dream.

These literal boys, those recognized as perpetrators in the school shootings, encounter and act out excessive states of rage and aggression in the absence of mechanisms of containment or inhibition, in other words, in the absence of the Goddess archetype. After reading Woodman's note to his high school peer (and to society), I understand that he was unable to transform or inhibit his personal indigestible rage and thus, he concretized it, a mad tragedy that appears to play out in many other school shootings. I also acknowledge that many children and adolescents experience rage yet are not destructive to others. It seems that a simultaneous psychopathy is present when such tragedies occur. When we look more closely at the word psychopathy, we see psyche (the Greek for soul) and pathos (the Greek for illness), arriving at the same place as that of a sickened soul.

Unfortunately, it is our schools—reflections of the larger culture—that have marginalized the archetypal feminine, the Goddess. Because she has been cast into the dark place of repression and denial, she can't transform excesses of rage and hate. How can we understand this denial of the feminine impulse in schools? We see this marginalization in school environments that focus on one-sided, outdated traditions, like sending messages that overvalue the hero-athlete—any student of any gender who wins fame through competition rather than collaboration. At the same time, microcultures grow within the schools, often resulting in the scapegoating of those youngsters who become devalued and are experienced as wimps, gays, lesbians, transgenders, dweebs, weirdoes, losers, Goths, and schoolboys. These scapegoated groups carry shadow projections requiring a counterresponse in terms of adult leadership.

Much has been said about educators pressured by political agendas, who surrender to policies that result in the loss of the archetypal feminine: art, music, counseling programs, and reparation initiatives. When schools are pressured financially, programs that foster creative, relational, and collaborative ways of experiencing the world are seen as expendable, unfortunately providing a good example of an undervaluation of the feminine in a patriarchal structure.

What if the sociocultural pressures of our students were met with authentic responses, which contain and transform (as the Goddess contains and transforms Dionysus' excesses)? What if curricula development seriously addressed and developed relational and creative capacities as well as academic skills? This requires time, focus, and financial support. How much different might Luke Woodman's experience have been if his feelings of hate and rage had been met with an effective healing program like the many programs that borrow from Native American peace practices? What if teachers and community members had engaged Woodman and his peers who bullied him, in specific, effective social justice programs and methods? In Beyerbach and Davis (Eds.) (2011), *Activist Art in Social Justice Pedagogy: Engaging Students in Glocal Issues through the Arts*, exemplary activist programs are described. Though fewer resources were available in 1997, they are available now, needing only brave educators and communities to embrace them.

All of these changes would signal a valuing of the Goddess. By this I mean that valuing the feminine principle requires conversations, and especially, direct initiatives aimed at inclusiveness and effective response to cultural wounding. Valuing the Goddess calls for consideration of issues of war and peace within a frame of death and life, rather than through a sole masculine expression of "higher values" like nationalism, and freedom, thereby bloating an expanded military agenda. The Goddess experiences war as destructive and real, affecting a multicultural world; she brings shadow motivations, like greed, to the table for thoughtful debate. These goddess perspectives need to balance the patriarchal attitude, which defines the school curriculum, usually by overvaluing science, math, and technology (intending that the nation will stay ahead in a competitive—masculine—rather than a collaborative—feminine—process).

## TRANSITION AND THE DARK GODDESS

A final question arises: why does this dream visit now? As archetypal dreams often visit at critical phases of the dreamer's life, this dream series of shootings can be seen as visiting the dreaming nation at a time when she is (without full conscious awareness) undergoing a major change. By example, her identity is transiting from a nation of economic and political superiority to a nation already merged with others—a part of world culture. She has not yet come to an awareness of how these changes have already altered her identity in terms of shifted autonomy, power, and economic status. As a leader nation jettisoned into the 3rd millennium, she, like the boys she dreams, is in a critical life phase, not the least of which is a transforming national psyche in which the Dark Goddess is emerging. We might remember that all archetypes contain both positive and negative elements. The archetypal feminine does not respond with her positive aspects when she is devalued, as she is in the current patriarchy. As I described above, in school cultures she has been forced too long to live a shadow experience.

In imagining the current violence as shadow, Betty Meador's (1994) words aptly describe the nation's negative feminine aspect: raging harpy, vicious, violent, and ruthless. It may be surprising to consider that these aspects are also at play in this complex dream. It is important to note that we are not speaking about literal or personal women, but about the dark aspect of the repressed collective feminine consciousness of the nation. With the Goddess we need to embrace both light and dark aspects. That is the new challenge. If she and her consort remain unconscious, they will energize destructive impulses as we all too clearly see. When the masculine and the feminine manifest in balance, harmony becomes possible.

Analyst and researcher Marion Woodman (1990) writes that it is this *conscious* feminine that can alter the course of environmental disregard. When she lives in the cultural consciousness, in the light, her gift is extraordinary:

the ability to repair and nurture not just school culture but also the earth. As the Great Mother, she is ontologically grounded in matter. In light of her promise, one must see the violence with which she thrusts herself from the bowels of a nation as a problem of societal neglect, a problem that can be resolved. Until then, both men and women suffer. The culture has the opportunity to hold a weighty reality to the light: our nation, like our schools, is *both* a playground *and* a dreamscape that expresses a destructive shadow.

## THE DREAM'S MEANING

This dream has presented a choice here: to provide hospitality to these images or to pretend that the imaginal is not present. All of you who have read to this point in the story have already made your choice. You have chosen to consider, to wonder about six streams of understanding emerging from the depths: (1) Guns in the hands of children may well be indigestible to national soul. (2) Overvaluing of the masculine power principle in schools supports marginalization and creates destructive imbalance. (3) Society must reclaim wholesome and meaningful initiatory rituals. (4) Repression of the feminine results in a failure to contain and transform excesses of aggression and hate. (5) Alienated boys risk identification with Nietzsche's place in the culture as a postmodern sacrificial figure. (6) A rising, and most unhappy Goddess consciousness requires acknowledgement, a move that supports positive transformation.

Perhaps this conversation and these understandings might allow us to stop pretending that only "evil" boy shooters are responsible for what seems at first glance, meaningless chaos. We are better positioned to open our societal eyes, just as 16-year-old Luke Woodman asked us to do in his poignant note, in 1997. Though he will remain incarcerated, at least until he is 65 years of age, we can respond to him with compassion (from the Greek, to be with in suffering) by changing the way we respond and fail to respond to the marginalized in school cultures.

## AFFECTS AND BELIEFS IN THE IMAGINAL FIELD

Analysis, as well as synthesis, is one of the processes by which I find meaning in my lived life. As I wrote the story called A Nation Dreams Its Violence, including its facts, and interpretations, I wondered, "What was initially and personally occurring in the imaginal realm, as I watched the news reports, and read the many articles that flooded the popular press while this phenomenon presented itself? What was my personal experience that both allowed the interpretation and impelled me to take refuge in it—from what threatened to be an overwhelming and deconstructing experience?

With the passage of time (1996–2015), I'm able to better explore the experience, which occurred beneath the analysis. The initial response was primarily, and initially, a feminine one, meaning I intuitively, randomly, and emotionally "knew" all that later became the cultural dream interpretation story. The dream brought a visceral experience: the chaos of unfolding events: shooting after shooting, multiple scenarios, and descriptions of tragic, yet contemptuous boy-faces in the act of murder. Before the analysis, before the interpretation, and before the scholarly research, I experienced, in both psyche and soma, pathos (from the Greek for suffering). Through a vague physical agitation, much like feeling "wired" in the aftermath of a car accident, I repeatedly experienced love unfulfilled, a nation's failure to embrace her children with relatedness, acceptance, and safety.

As I witnessed news reports and read articles in the press, I experienced what can best be described as undifferentiated rage, manifested in a state of unremitting irritation and a shadowy energy, which paced within a cage-like space. The rage was not at all conscious but seemed to reside deep within, like my own muted labor contractions after morphine was administered years ago, to stop the process of birthing in an attempt to preclude a too early birth. I could feel the pain; it was present, but resided far below and simply did not hurt. I also experienced bombarding and repetitive thoughts (i.e., how could these youngsters look so young and innocent, hunched over and subdued as they are hauled off by the police and still be filled with uncontainable, murderous rage, and contempt? How could such opposing states reside in the same young individuals without a host of adults noticing and intervening?).

I was aware that deeper, more complex realities within the phenomenon were being muted by a patriarchal attitude. I felt that what my feminine consciousness experienced—knowing the weapons and the shooters as part of a literal dream and also as illuminating dream characters—would likely be marginalized by the societal masculine attitude, even though that one-sided masculine way of existence, if not unchecked, would kill the world. From my years of being a woman in the world, I knew that the society would articulate this phenomenon through an outdated matrix of reality. I thus witnessed the old pattern of scapegoating; the problem became framed in terms of violent videos and Game Boy products, the breakdown of the family, or the too-narrow focus on the criminality of the shooters. What was missing was a collaborative, deep, and courageous look at the cultural underpinnings of the tragedies. As a teacher leader, I felt what seemed like impenetrable walls of the patriarchal structures (and have shared my thoughts earlier on this issue of balance). Most importantly, I felt existential guilt because it seemed that the task at hand, to balance the masculine and feminine, outsized my personal ability to fulfill its requirements.

Initially, none of these feelings were conscious, logical, or structured in language. As I experienced matter and mind, profoundly mediated by the organ of imagination, I experienced images that before the organizing function of interpretation (meaning making), seemed to float around my being like the flat images in medieval paintings before modern perspective offered a sense of depth and distance. My initial experience was such that there was no sense of order, no category, no hierarchy of moral affront to the images—metal weapons, blood, grief stricken faces, and coffins. Affect seemed to have a life of its own, entering the imaginal space as yet another image. The sound of contemptuous and maniacal laughter became the final, loud figure. These images—nontemporal, nonlocal, and nonspacial, alive before the analysis conceptualized, or ego relativized them— simply hovered, like flying saucers within the imaginal space of my woman's experience, chasing away so much that comprised my life.

In those early days in which affect dominated, I felt grief, fear, and a muted sense of impending doom, not as conscious and naked feeling, but as nameless dread. I saw distortions and contortions of a nation in collapse, much as I felt the distortion and contortion of my woman's body when my son was being born prematurely, destined (I was told) to die. As a woman I felt the terror of a nation inadequate to the task of containing and nurturing its boy-children, thus unleashing a danger on all her children. This is how I, as a woman, experienced life events that patriarchal consciousness reduced to sound bites.

Within the limited consciousness of this imaginal space, I attempted to speak to others in my educational environment. For example, I went one day to a school district as a consultant on sexuality issues, on a day that coincided with the murder of a student who happened to be a member of a marginalized group within the school—he was a gang member and a boy of color. I found myself in a leadership role, attempting to resurrect the boy's dignity as a soulful person, and leading the group to a healing stance in terms of how these teachers would guide the student body toward reparation and renewal. Though my contribution and insights were met with enthusiasm and connection by my colleagues, they seemed a small contribution when compared to the task at hand—restoring meaning and connectedness to all students within the school community. All this while, the cultural dream images were percolating within my imaginal realm. Such professional responding, while only somewhat effective, seemed to ground my ego and to keep me psychologically organized.

That teachers change the course of individual lives was (and is) a core belief for me. Many give a lifetime of commitment and devotion, in a world in which money and power, not vocation, are valued. Yet I worked within a humbling reality that beyond the individual classroom experience, we educators do little to change education's cultural machine. I witnessed this frustration at the public education level as well as at the university level where, through scholarship and partnership, educators participate more fully in the deconstruction and reconstruction of assumptions about students and schools. In my view, at the academic level too, systemic change is often impermanent or inadequate.

In the very early days in which the national dream entered my personal landscape, it was my belief that in the end the study of Western thought continued to emerge as essentially a masculine project. Even now, one studies Western thought and development by knowing Plato, Aristotle, Augustine, Newton, Kant, Einstein, and Bohr (all men) (Tarnas, 1991). I could easily name modern American inventors, statesmen, or scientists (all men). The occasional mention of a woman here and there—Tubman, Stanton, Roosevelt, Meir, (Indira) Gandhi, Thatcher—continues to underscore the relative miniscule story of women's contributions. They seem, too often, to enter the story (his-story) as afterthoughts, as crumbs thrown at feminist critique. It is only since the emergence of the second wave of the feminist movement that women's gnosis is permeating linguistics, science, psychoanalysis, and natural science; epistemology is slowly changing because of this feminist contribution to Western thought.

Perhaps most important to my experience as I navigated this phenomenon of school shootings was my ability to access the mundus imaginalis. It was the ability to see intuitively and to relate imaginatively to the unfolding events that gave me access to this in-between world of imagination, that soulful and illuminating realm. It was painful, but more importantly it was real. That the world is realized through the depth of imaginative seeing is its promise. The issue is not really whether what one sees is attractive or gruesome, but rather that such vision of the real is grounded in the feminine (the home of the imaginal field), an idea shared by other scholars: Whitmont (2001), Tarnas (1991), and Woodman (1990).

One of the questions threading through this book is, "Does engagement with the imaginal realm cause it to manifest?" In this story of the cultural dream, I observe that for me, engagement with the imaginal causes it to become more fully illuminated, more real, more colorful, replete with informative figures, and deeply enlivened. It is as if the imaginal is always present but requires conscious intention to host her, in order to achieve visibility, meaning—as in the example of my experience within this story—that one must choose to contemplate the events as imaginal reality as well as phenomena of mind and matter. In the act of providing hospitality, the dream's images become boldfaced as the "bold" font on a computer causes certain selected words to become more visible, more valued in the discourse. So too does the engagement of and attention to the imaginal drama of school violence cause me to see beyond the veil of an in-between world, even though such seeing is limited by the degree to which I am able to tolerate the disorientating onslaught of negative affect and somatic disturbance that accompany even intermittent consciousness of the real.

## THE CONSTELLATED CULTURAL FIELD

In the dream/story above, I have shared the views of Woodman (1990), Tarnas (1991), and Whitmont (2001), as well as my own, that a cultural deconstruction is underway, resulting from a 5,000-year repression of the archetypal feminine. For them and for me, it seems clear that the repressed feminine is rising and will be made conscious, or the fate of the nation (and the earth herself) is at imminent risk.

I see this feminine figure manifested in the constellated field. Her anger is understandable; even many personal women, for whom union with the Goddess would seem most expected, did not desire her, not until the feminist project awakened a world to the cultural peril that her absence generated.

I wrote in Chapter 2 about the archetypal character Ereshkigal, who was enraged and played havoc on my own life until I acknowledged her and acted out of a consciousness informed by her presence. This is what is happening on a national level.

This predominant figure in the field is the archetype of the postmodern Goddess, yet another face of the Goddess. As the archetypes are multivocal, multivalent, and infinite, she is born out of the new world order and is a new dimension of the devouring Goddess. Just as the ancient Goddess devoured Dionysus as a means of transformation and containment (Whitmont, 2001), this modern goddess devours the young Dionysian boy shooters.

I agree with Tarnas (1991) that on an archetypal level, the development of differentiated cultural ego is a positive outcome of the 5,000-year period in which the masculine principal was overvalued. This overvaluing of the masculine has resulted in advances in genetics, the microchip, Newtonian, then quantum physics, and democracy. These testimonies to consciousness were paid with the currency of a disowned earth, disregard for instinct, intuition, and a desouled cosmos, a high price that is now being mediated by the re-membering of the feminine in both men and women. The movement towards reclaiming and subsequent transformation of the postmodern Goddess is being led by new voices of women and men in linguistics, economics, social justice, psychology, and education, virtually all fields of human development.

Of the contributions of the women who are postmodern agents, deconstructing that which the cultural masculine has distorted, Tarnas (1991) writes

> New and powerful insights have emerged from the work of Rosemary Ruether, Mary Daly, Beatrice Bruteau, Joan Chamberlain Engelsman, and Elain Pagels in religious studies; of Marija Gimbutas in archaeology; of Carol Gilligan in moral and developmental psychology; of Jean Baker Miller and Nancy Chodorow in psychoanalysis; of Stephanie de Voogd and Barbara Eckman in epistemology; of a host of

feminine scholars in history, anthropology, sociology, jurisprudence, economics, ecology, ethics, aesthetics, literary theory, and cultural criticism. (p. 408)

Tarnas (1991), a man and scholar for whom the feminine, as well as the masculine, is a personal, embodied aspect of self, writes of the feminist critical perspective as possessing transformative dimensions:

> Considered as a whole, the feminist perspective and impulse has brought forth perhaps the most vigorous, subtle, and radically critical analysis of conventional intellectual and cultural assumptions in all of contemporary scholarship. No academic discipline or area of human experience has been left untouched by the feminist reexamination of how meanings are created and preserved, how evidence is selectively interpreted and theory molded with mutually reinforcing circularity, how particular rhetorical strategies and behavioral styles have sustained male hegemony, how women's voice remained unheard through centuries of social and intellectual male dominance, how deeply problematic consequences have ensued from masculine assumptions about reality, knowledge, nature, society, the divine. (p. 408)

It is within this critical attitude that the postmodern Goddess is creating new frameworks within which the contemporary mind can experience less dichotomized realities. This diverse and collective feminist voice is the voice of archetypal transformation. In the way of the feminine, feared because she is the Goddess of life and death, this archetype is devouring not only a culture's adolescent boy shooters, but also male hegemony. This immerging figure in the imaginal field is, for me, the solution to our cultural dream in which boy children murder in the schools. It is her emergence that psyche asks a nation to support. She is the answer to an ensouled nation's compensation dream. Her archetypal impulse—in the scholarship and lived lives of women and the growing number of men who invite her to conscious expression—leads the way to the corrected cultural attitude. Her realization has begun and requires cultural tending and hospitality.

****************

## PROLOGUE TO CRONES IN THE SHADOWLANDS

In the second story of Chapter 3, "Crones in the Shadowlands," I explore, through the telling of one particular moment of my life, another aspect of women's experience, that dwells in the shadowy realm of societal consciousness, that of the Crone archetype.

As the archetypal Crone becomes constellated in my life, active in the unconscious field, she appears to me in the person of a yoga instructor and in two figures within a significant and life-changing dream. In this final story, I share her emergence in my waking and dream worlds and my analysis of the dream in which her symbolic figures caused me to integrate her consciously into my woman's life. I then look more deeply at the affects, beliefs, and imaginal figures who enter my lived life as her consciousness bubbles forth.

In Walker (1985), the crone archetype is the face of the feminine that can best be described as a woman of age, power, and wisdom. The Crone represents the power of the tribal matriarch. She is the embodiment of shaman energies. Walker (1985) writes that she established the cyclic system of perpetual becoming, "whereby every temporary living form in the universe blends eventually into every other form, nothing is unrelated, and there can be no hierarchy of better or worse, We and They" (p. 14). Thus, the Crone's philosophical system is profoundly opposed to that which structures the world view of modern society. She is an old woman who acknowledges no master.

## CRONES IN THE SHADOWLANDS

Today I went to yoga class. The teacher is in her 70s. She is wiry, agile, and full, like a summer bouquet, with kindness and strength. My heart responds to her age, her face, and her ministrations to her students. She also is given to bluntly owning her inclinations. For example, beyond her yoga work, she hosts drummings, ceremonies in which participants rhythmically chant, play instruments, go within; they then share spiritual unfoldings, such as visions. This crone woman is "not nice" in stating who is invited and who is not; she is simply unequivocal. She is open to those whom she believes will enrich the ritual and is clear that she does the inviting and no one else. Because the Crone is not bound by societal constrictions such as rules of etiquette, she has no eruptions of unconscious cruelty, no nasty tail that strikes before she thinks. The crone is powerful but can be trusted. She is neither controlled nor controlling.

She began the class by guiding us in moistening our hands and massaging each other's feet. This is how it should be; this is a reclaiming of the goddess mysteries. We were women healing other women, women not paralyzed with fear of being in our own nature—matter, flesh, and sensation. This is a move to a cultural consciousness in which the goddess manifests in a gymnasium where women join in full relationship—body and soul. For me, the foot massage was not sexual but sensual. It was pleasing and sacred. Because the temenos created by this ritual was built within the walls of our city's YMCA—the Young Men's Christian Association, where I as a very young girl first learned to sew, and where classes years ago were very gender defined and conservative—I knew that a deeply embedded paradigm shift is unfolding.

Having experienced women in such bodily expression, I went to bed feeling safe and contained, able to welcome, in dreamtime, still another face of archetypal womanhood, the Crone. Such connection with the Crone archetype is rare for me. As my woman's journey continues, her consciousness is not fully developed. I notice a tendency within to keep the crone at bay. For me, the Crone holds the unattractive face of the goddess, the potential for dark power and magic. She is not pretty or young or pleasing of body. She does not value gentleness, for her a waste of time. One can sometimes detect a faint sour vulva scent as she approaches; washing too much does not interest her.

Her consciousness is expressed in fairy tales (Grimm's, 1972). In "The Goose Girl at the Well" (pp. 725–734), she is not the "too good mother" but the old snaggle-toothed hag, a witch, who cares for the lost girl child in the woods. Her attitude toward men is unencumbered with romantic illusions. She is a no-nonsense wise woman who does not mince words. In "The Goose Girl at the Well," she pushes and puffs mockingly at the young man in the story, The young gentleman will not carry what I, an old woman have so often dragged along. "You are ready with fine words, but when it comes to be earnest, you want to take to your heels. Why are you standing loitering there?" she continued; "step out." (p. 276)

And to the goose girl, a princess in disguise, whom the crone has cared for 3 years, she brings the same no-nonsense approach. In the story, the girl finds out that the old woman who had cared for her is leaving, knowing that her work with the girl is done. The girl cries and does not want the hag to leave; "Tell me what is about to happen?"

In this highly charged moment, the Crone response is typically pointed and assertive,

> I tell you again, do not hinder me in my work. Do not say a word more, go to your chamber, take the skin off your face, and put on the silken gown, which you had on when you came to me, and then wait in your chamber until I call you. (p. 732)

It is she whose consciousness pushes us to do the soul work at hand—sorting messes that common living brings; it is she who will not suffer fools.

Her consciousness demands that we see what must be seen. The Crone sees through the seductive, charming man, who in the end is a cad. The smooth-talking politician hinting at a sharing of power is exposed as a liar. In the foreign film, *The Red Violin* (Girard, 1998), she appeared as Cesca, presenting amulets and bones to the beautiful pregnant Madame, saying, "If your husband spits on them, it will help." (She makes reference to a safe birth.) When the young woman resists, "My husband is tired of spitting," Cesca contemptuously offers the crone's response, "Spitting is what men are good for," signifying a consciousness that is not patriarchal, not overvaluing of the masculine. At this early point in *The Red Violin*, the issue at hand is for a safe birth and the well-being of the maiden and her child. The young woman is more concerned with her husband's leanings. This represents the consciousness of the woman who wants to please her man (a consciousness also addressed in my memoir to follow).

In the cultural imagination, the Crone is not social and generally dwells apart, on the fringe of the village. In fairy tales, the townspeople seek her out when the children are lost or the monster comes; she is a source of wisdom today, the creator of potions. Shaman energy dwells in her realm; she easily outwits patriarchal fixity and neglect. In the Middle Ages, millions of women were burned and drowned as witches (Shinoda Bolen, 1991); it was the Crone's wisdom and healing powers that were feared. It was her archetypal impulse that was hunted down and murdered. It was she who entered my own dreamscape last night and shoved me about.

I share this dream and the gnosis it brought to underscore the power of Crone consciousness, to illustrate the value, which only her no-nonsense attitude can bring, and also to bid her entrance to my woman's story. She is magic and sees beyond Eros' need for companionship of the other, beyond a women's need to be sexually embraced. She is no longer desired by men, no longer desires them, and thus carries the symbology of an unwashed vulva; its stink spits in the face of sexual possibility. What pleasure she gets, she happily and toothlessly gives herself, thank you very much.

## BRINGING UP THE DEAD

I am in an old house that I share with a man. It is the house I lived in as a child in a coal-mining town. Many old Polish women live on this street. Their presence is everywhere in the dream, they garden, cook and gossip. They are bent, large, and strong; if they do anything well, it is to endure. In the dream, as in the reality of my childhood, I do not see them in loving intimate relationship with men, the men in their lives are long dead, drunkards, or simply ignored.

As we move about our house I sense my man's soul energy and think of the movie Deliverance, a macabre film in which some hillbillies who live in the deep southern back country capture two men on a canoe trip. They torment the men in the manner of budding psychopathic boys: cornering them, laughing at their fear, and then sodomizing them.

In the dream, I choose not to consciously confront this hillbilly aspect of my man, wanting only to keep him happy, to please him so that I will be kept in relationship with him. In the dream I am numb to the affect in our home. He lumbers about telling me to go out to the yard and dig up the dead body of our 8-year-old daughter, he wants to see her. I do not want to do this and pretend to be occupied, not to hear, but he—stupid, dressed in a sleeveless undershirt and shorts—follows me about, beer bottle in hand, whining and demanding.

Finally I sigh and with a contempt that defends against my own weakness, I go outside, to the shed. Grabbing the shovel, I go to the place where our daughter lies and begin to bring up the dirt, clod-by-clod, clump by heavy clump. I am numb, feeling only irritation, but somewhere far away, a thought, born by rising dust, whispers, "Betrayal."

It is then that I notice that two neighbor ladies have come out to their back porch to see what I am doing. They are never embarrassed at

being in my business, all business is theirs, gossip and interference their daily bread. Gray hair crowns them both, pulled back in a tight knot on one, hanging loose and hag-like on the other. Each is round and hunched and dry. Their androgynous leathery faces peer at me. They begin to cackle at me, "Don't do for him." I stop for a moment and see the longhaired woman light her pipe. She puffs slow and free and snickers to her friend, "She digs the 8-year-old child from the grave." I tell them that my husband is not so bad and wants this. They are loud in their disagreement, nipping at me with their words, shoving me about. I am paralyzed between wanting to heed them and wanting to dig. I wake confused and exhausted. (Harrell, Dream Journal, 1999)

It is my habit to work with dreams, looking for an attitude, a behavior a part of personality that wants to be seen, that without psyche's image remains hidden, unacknowledged. The gift in every dream is the possibility of discovery. I often do not like what I discover. It is unconscious for a reason, masking that which lives within me, the unpleasant, the difficult, and the unattractive and weak, threatening to offend my own identity as a worthy woman.

## I-N-T-E-R-R-E-D

And so I began unraveling the dream riddle, making associations, turning the images upside down, right side up, playing with the words within, asking myself what had recently occurred, and so on. I had just spoken with my ex-husband on the phone. I have not seen him for 4 years. He is a dignified man, educated. This dream could not be about him. I usually explore dream images as part of my own personality; I try first to look within.

I remembered too that as I wrote hours before retiring for the evening that I seemed to use the word "entered" repeatedly, yet each time I tried to write the letters my pen scrawled out i-n-t-e-r-r-e-d. I asked even then what this uninvited word wanted of me, but found no answer. And now in the dream's image, the word returns. I am disturbing my interred daughter.

The crones are there too, representing an attitude of seeing the truth of things, not being fooled by callings of the heart, of charades or "nice" gestures. Their message is unequivocal, "Don't do for him." They see me clearly, digging my child from her grave, her resting place.

My literal child is not dead; she is alive and well. I remembered then that I mentioned to my former spouse, her stepfather, the night before, about her successful audition, her getting a job as vocalist in an orchestra. How, I thought, am I digging her up? What 8-year-old part of my own part of personality am I digging up? This is about the dead; it is about interment and doing an unnatural act. This dream, I suspected, was about crone consciousness calling out to me to see some macabre attitude or behavior. I knew this from many years of dream work.

As the dream feeling and images were tossed and turned, a truth came to me that sickened me. My former husband's outward self is the aspect that's dignified and educated, yet my psychological experience of his inner world, seemed more like that of the character in the dream. And perhaps, more importantly, the dream's husband image was also an aspect of my own animus.

I remember working so long and hard to grow a strong and healthy animus figure, my own soul, from the shriveled, distasteful character that it used to be. Over 4 years, I have mined my dreams and witnessed a growing inner image of a masculine self increasingly free of soul problems. Yet from time to time, an internal problematic animus image returns. So this dream husband was both an image of my own weak experience of self and an intrapsychic experience of my former spouse's unconscious energy.

On the day before I had the dream, I remembered that on the phone, I told my ex about my daughter, his step daughter, who holds a soft spot in his heart, as he has been a "dad" to her since she was 7 years old. He needs, I fantasize, this part of the relationship that has undergone 4 years of his refusal to see her, to call, to be "dad." I realized now that for both of them, the father–daughter relationship has shrunken from neglect and a cold turning away. He buried their relationship and put her away in the deep underground, a soul underworld. His lack of relating, involvement, and support as she struggled to make the adult world her own, killed a part of her that trusted, that felt contained, that felt loved by him.

And there I was just hours before, pretending to give him news of her, when really I was using her, to create an attachment between us—an unfortunate though unconscious attempt on my part to cling to this man, whom my orphaned part of soul continued to want.

I remembered now a faraway and unheeded twinge of guilt as I told him of her new position. It felt much like the whispered word, "Betrayal" in the dream. I knew what I was doing, but pretended I did not. I was digging her up and serving her up for my own end. This is why, I know, the word interred kept creeping from my pen. I am acutely aware that many mothers, in small incremental ways, betray their daughters for security, a man's presence, for promise of their own containment by the masculine.

The soul of a word lies in its etymology. Interred has its root in the Latin terra or interrare, to put in the earth (Barnhart, 1995, p. 393).

In Becker (1994):

> The EARTH is in contrast to SKY; the earth is usually interpreted as being feminine, passive, dark; it often appears in mythology as a feminine deity sometimes compared with the womb, related to the Great Mother, goddess of life and death. (p. 92)

The dream images demand that this dead child's interment be undisturbed, calling, perhaps, for a state in which undeveloped cosmic feminine consciousness be allowed to rest in the realm of the deep maternal. All that enters the earth is birthed from her in time. This symbology may point to the return of a feminine consciousness that is grounded in the chthonic, the deep, and the goddess mysteries.

From a more personal perspective, my own daughter's relationship and betrayal by a literal stepfather must lie undisturbed within the womb of the Great Mother, so that she can experience in her own natural way the life, death, life cycle of the world. The resolution of this father/daughter breach must be what it is until her soul's longing, or his, rises it up from the depths.

Importantly too, individuation is a deeper look at my own actions. I have struggled, for the most part successfully, not to participate in maternal betrayal, understanding it as the greatest archetypal breach. The potential for this kind of breach, to the degree that it lives in me, would want to, need to, hide as shadow. Marie-Louis von Franz writes (1996) that "in fairy tales, the problem of the shadow is intertwined with the problem of the animus" (p. 163), true also of this dream/life situation which the unconscious brought to me, psyche's own form of the fairy tale.

## A GRAVE BETRAYAL

It is the nature of Crone consciousness to call out the truth, shoving me at it and it at me, not giving two cents about my aversion toward the capacity of betrayal within myself. Even the Crone's dream gesture of blowing smoke was an image of "blowing smoke," the colloquial term for fakery. The Crones were clear. In my one act that night on the phone, I had fallen into that dark place. Even now I want to defend, saying it was not a grave betrayal. And the Crones scream, even in my waking state, "Look at the image woman, if you see nothing at all you must see that it was a grave betrayal." There is no hiding from these old women. Most betrayals of mothers are not bold and one dimensional like Judas betraying Jesus, with one act, one kiss. No, most woman betray their children clod-by-clod, clump by heavy clump. I knew the Crones would not rest until I took personal responsibility, creating an embodied and conscious shift to a place of integrity.

And so, like the girl in the fairy tales, I began the work of sorting, preparing a place of hospitality, cleaning up. And as in the fairy tales, the Crones now move on to other business. We know also that in the fairy tales they do return, do check to see if the work is done.

I needed to discuss with my own strong and beautiful daughter what her wishes were where this man was concerned and to honor them, to allow her to tell him of her evolving life or not. It is all her choice, not mine. I was required, also, to tell her that I had shared her success with him, and that that was not my place. She agreed with a gentle acknowledgement and even support of my need to look at this part of myself. And so in the privacy of my own soul work, I confronted that part of my being that was undeveloped and stupid, and that ran around in an old tank top, digging up the dead because I was needy.

My beer bottle was the muddled anesthetized way in which I lumbered about, not seeing the harm I was doing, acting out my lack of healthy animus function by carrying the corpse of my daughter's relationship to him. This illumination leaves my ex-husband to do his own work or not. It must be his choice also.

I tell this story not to expose my darker side, but to speak the truth. Von Franz wrote of the shadow (1996), "the shadow is a low fellow." She continues, "If he can get returns without hard work, he cannot help not working. To be able not to go the easy way is a sign of great self-discipline and culture" (p. 140). None of us can afford to close our conscious attitude from the interference of the Crone. We need her ability to look with harsh reality at our motivation. When our weakness overwhelms consciousness, we must call to the Crone, for her independence and ruthlessness.

Shadow figures, like other intrapsychic images, are sent by the self as an offering for our individuation. They need not be shunned or feared. They bring opportunity for consciousness and deep wisdom. Not gazing at them only encourages them toward mischief. The aim is to hold their images in consciousness, to integrate that part of self that they represent so that life might be lived with balance. For me, the integration of the crone's ruthlessness and aggression is difficult; without her qualities of being, it is too difficult to write well; the work sounds tentative. It is difficult to attain goals without leaking vitality if Crone consciousness is absent. So each achievement—like the new-found way in which I approach relationship with my former husband—is precious. More importantly, the joining of consciousness with outward enactment brings the wholeness that the work of individuation seeks.

## AFFECTS AND BELIEFS

At the time in my life when the Crone began to manifest, I had been separated for 4 years, and was legally and emotionally ending my marriage with my second husband. There was no significant male figure in my life professionally or personally. At 52 years of age, I had just moved to New York from California, a move which brought closure to a period in my life in which my husband's choices relative to climate, professional positions, purchases, and investments of money and time, in my opinion, had played more of a role in my life than was healthy. Nonetheless, within this union, there were many soulful gifts to me, and to us as a couple because of his family leadership, for many of our years together, and because he carried much of the burden of family responsibilities, I was free to grow professionally and spiritually, during a period of about 7 years. But that period had begun to collapse several years before we separated, and in some parts of my being, this latest period of closure brought relief, a sense of freedom and agency.

Emotionally, I was free of all the relationships that had defined and organized me. I was no longer mothering, nurturing, providing the relational ground for a family. Thus, I was both lost and powerfully, intoxicatingly free. I was living the life of the Crone: my life was unencumbered, familiar with and empowered by my experience and talents as an educator, as an unfolding mature woman, and I was moving into the realm of the healer as a psychological intern. As a doctoral student in a clinical psychology program with an emphasis in depth psychology, I was being initiated into the depths of soulwork, moving into "new" shamanism.

I had, 3 months before my Crone dream, taken an exciting position as a full-time assistant professor with the School of Education at State University of New York, Oswego. I felt appreciated as a woman there, and also professionally and personally valued and supported. I was welcomed into an academic milieu in which many men and women lived out of balanced masculine and feminine aspects of self. Cooperation rather than competition filled our world, and an attitude of educational passion was part of our initiatives, our teaching, and our scholarship.

My affect was a pool of dichotomies: currents of the orphan, the longing woman, the empowered writer, the independent and joyful friend, the abundantly successful and appreciated mother of a young woman imbued my emotional world. I was a becoming woman, the wise woman. I was on the threshold of menopause, that time of pausing from the realm of men.

The streams of intellectual, soulful, and bodily aspects of my life reminded me of the postmodern world itself (Tarnas, 1991). Daily life for me was anxiety producing because I was constantly being deconstructed and reconstructed: I lived in a world of many dynamic and ambiguous realities, the old paradigms that had structured my life, no longer worked. My interactions with university colleagues caused me to challenge assumptions of class, gender, ageism, ableism, and race at an accelerated rate that caused me to feel, at times, emotionally, intellectually, and soulfully dizzy. And yet my life was characterized by a freedom that seemed appropriate to the multidimensional, multivocal woman I was becoming.

Thus, my emotional state was one in which Crone energy emerged within a matrix of positive and negative affect and a somewhat over-animated state of death and resurrection, suggesting that familiar move toward an undifferentiated ego state that seems intermittently present in other encounters in the imaginal, in which I participate.

## THE CONSTELLATED IMAGINAL FIELD

The central figures in this story in which Crone consciousness is brought out of the shadows and integrated into my woman's life are the two Crones in the dream, and also the yoga instructor at the YMCA. In the imaginal field I, too, am a central figure because of my physical and psychological readiness to enter the lived life of the Crone. My life circumstance, my perimenopausal body, and unconscious actions were linked with, but did not cause, the archetypal Crone to manifest in the imaginal field. I claim that these circumstances and unconscious impulses allowed a personal recognition and familiarity with the Crone, by which I joined with her as she manifested. We were two ends of the psychoid archetype within the imaginal field.

I want to emphasize that in the imaginal realm, time is a continuing birthing, a re-commencement (Corbin, 1960/1989); there is no past, therefore, I know, in an intuitive, soulful way that as I re-imagine the Crone in my story and in my life, all the other women who have welcomed her, have embodied her, and have lived through her consciousness, are in the field with the Crone and me. I feel the presence of Helen, my maternal grandmother, and Sadie, my paternal grandmother. I see my own mother, Josephine; my sisters JoAnn, Michelle, Marella, Camilla, Connie, and Chris; my dear friend in her 70s, Mrs. Hessinger; Nana, my first husband's mother; my step-mother Cecilia; and the delightful, outrageous Aunt Tina who you will meet in the following story. Present also are Aunts Gloria, Madelyn, Ida, Mary Ann, Betsy, Irene, Charlotte, and Loretta. This imaginal world is remarkable because of this sense of flexible space-time, which joins so many in the eternal, present moment of soul. Even the future is closer than in the realm of modernity. It's as if we Crone sisters already prepare the way for my daughter Lauren and nieces Sarah, Janell, Dana, April, Emilie, Katie, Alden, Danielle, Elizabeth, Kyra, and Aymie. Such a beloved circle of wise women—re-imagined and becoming—causes me to weep.

In my experience of the imaginal realm, it makes little difference whether a figure exists as a concrete, literal person (the yoga instructor, or myself), or as a vital, imaginal figure in the field (the crones in the dream). Imagination mediates the world of the senses and the world of the intellect. It is that mediating function of being (Corbin, 1961/1989) that produces the alchemy, in which I am one of several participants. It feels to me that in the domain of imagination, the lines blur between that which is a material/spiritual figure and an imaginal figure, just as imagination creates a new neither/nor reality between the realms of the sensible and the intellect.

As a figure in this imaginal field, my consciousness seems less dominated by ego than when I am in the realm of mind/body consciousness. I am far less an observing subject and far more a creating participant in

reality; in this sense, the ego seems relativized and reality expands. Paradoxically, ego consciousness is important in allowing my observing mind
to observe, lest I become overcome by the constellated archetype, or lose
the meaning of the dream. It is this role of ego as observer, mediated by
the imaginative faculty, that allows the dream interpretation. It is also the
ego's function to bring the transformed attitude into societal enactment,
meaning that in the case of my story, I needed ultimately to call my daughter and speak with her about what I had done, to take responsibility for the
betrayal, and to right my own path, my Tao.

The imaginal field in this story, like the field in other stories, is essentially
a place where I experience the presence of an Other, a creator of reality. To
explain this sense of the Other in the imaginal field, Tarnas (1991) writes:

> The bold conjectures and myths that the human mind produces in
> its quest for knowledge ultimately come from something far deeper
> than a purely human source. They come from the wellspring of nature
> itself, from the universal unconscious that is bringing forth through
> the human mind and human imagination its own gradually unfolding
> reality. (pp. 436–437)

For me, as for Tarnas (1991), this creative Other is the collective unconscious, working in this particular field of personal imaginal experience,
even as it simultaneously works in the fields of others to create a new paradigm whose pulse I feel in the world, a paradigm in whose unfolding I play
a small role, in the sense that the collective unconscious, the Other, seems
to be breaking through, to bring the notion of the *mundus imaginalis* to
societal consciousness, through inspiring such a study as this, and through
bringing others in connection with me to mirror the work.

In the story, the alchemy among the crones—in the dream and in my
yoga instructor—myself, and the other dream figures was also constructed
by this creative Other, the collective unconscious. Hillman's (1983) notion
of purposefulness, or *tellete*, that the unconscious has intentionality, supports my claim that the Other, or psyche, or soul, or Divine plays a deci-
sive and intentional part in this unfolding field. These figures in the field,
including the felt sense of the Other, are both figures in the unconscious
field, and also consciously perceived imaginal characters. In Ansbacher
(Ansbacher and Ansbacher, 1964), Adler clarifies this visible conscious/
unconscious dichotomy when he writes,

> "The unconscious…is not hiding away in some unconscious or subconscious recess of our minds, but is part of our consciousness, the significance of which we have not fully understood." (p. 232)

Thus, in the crone dream, after some interpretation, the archetypal field included crone figures, which became conscious and required bodily expression (mine) for fulfillment and enactment in reality. Once I became conscious of the crone figures' message, I then became the embodied Crone in relating to my daughter, and in relating to my former husband. It is not surprising that in the years that followed, he and I have never had occasion to speak to each other, meaning that the constellated field touched both of us, and allowed a link, which did not serve soul, to be broken.

I wish to end with a quote from Malleus Maleficarum (Whitmont, 2001). This text was compiled by two Dominican friars and authorized by Pope Innocent VIII as the judiciary standard, for the adjudication of witches. It was the standard of legal judgment from the 15th to the 17th century. I include it here because witches were and are especially feared for their wisdom and healing powers. Their genocide, a term aptly designated by psychiatrist Jean Shinoda Bolen (1991), is a reminder that to be a crone should not be romanticized in a patriarchal world view, such as that of our Western culture.

Cronehood is a serious responsibility, and to the degree that crones become visible in any patriarchy, they risk being victimized (Walker, 1985), as they have historically carried shadow projections for cultures who marginalize the feminine. The Crone is the carrier of power and authority for the feminine. She does not fear the masculine, nor is she daunted by hegemony. The Crone is needed in cultures whose history and attitudes towards women are marginalizing. Such marginalizing attitudes are clear in the following quotes from Malleus, as reported in Whitmont (2001):

> "According to Malleus, women are moved predominantly by intensity of affect and emotion. Their extremes of love or hate are generated by the "lust of the flesh," by possessiveness and jealousy. "More carnal than the man," they are, in fact, sexually insatiable, vain, pleasure-seeking liars and seducers, bent on deceiving in order to achieve their own ends. They are mentally and intellectually inferior, deficient and "feeble in mind and body"; of poor memory, "intellectually like children," over-credulous, superstitious, over-impressionable and suggestible, of "slippery tongue," undisciplined; indeed, altogether like an "imperfect animal." (p. 124)"

In closing, the archetypal field within my story and dream is a field in which Crone consciousness is predominant. Her consciousness alone has the strength to mediate the depths of the negative affect and beliefs described in the quote above, and yet remains in cultural shadow—a truth that has been articulated by feminist scholarship in many fields (Tarnus, 1991). She is a shadow figure in the broad culture, and was an archetypal shadow figure in my personal inner life.

In the story, the personal shadow figure became conscious, but there is no past in the imaginal realm; nothing is done or unchangeable. Therefore, consciousness must be rebirthed, re-created many times. Corbin (1989) writes, "While we believe that we are looking at what is past and unchangeable, we are in fact consummating our own future" (p. xxix). Thus, the unconscious personal crone will need to be brought to consciousness in my lived experience over and over. Her conscious birth and illumination will need to be re-membered, because for the soul, "all acts of understanding are so many re-iterations of events yet remains unconcluded" (Corbin, 1989, p. xxix).

\*\*\*\*\*\*\*\*\*\*\*\*\*\*\*\*

## LIGHT SHADOW

In this third story, titled "Aunt Tina: Sensual Goddess," I wish to highlight the notion of light shadow, which occurs when an individual represses talents or attitudes in an attempt to experience safety or to avoid responsibility. Unlike my memoir of the dreaming nation, this next story holds a much different tone and is a more personal account. "Aunt Tina: Sensual Goddess" is a story of lived exuberance and wholeness. For Aunt Tina the Goddess is not repressed, not in shadow; her story is a juxtaposition from so many women in the broader world. I give it as an example of what can be gained as more and more women embody the Sensual Goddess and live out of what cultural pressures would relegate to the shadows. Aunt Tina's sensual and vital life seems unusual for a woman of her time and therefore underscores the lived phenomenon of realized cultural light shadow, resurrected from the depths.

As men and women live out of a patriarchal theophany, the values of the God image require the embodiment of particular feminine behaviors and attitudes (those which support and protect the values of the patriarchy), whereas others are relegated to the shadows. For example, as women live out of the maternal feminine they are rewarded; living out of crone consciousness, however, has resulted in the genocide of millions of women in the Middle Ages (Shinoda Bolen, 1991). In today's postmodern culture, many women are achieving a re-construction of the Crone, celebrating her, and living out of her wise-woman energies.

To live sensually, joyfully, within a matrix of pleasure and contained excess is living out of the Sensual Goddess archetype. My aunt does this because she is a delightful and vibrant woman. Many years ago, because her husband lost his leg in a mining accident, she was required to develop and live out of masculine capacities (i.e., becoming the family financial provider, which in the 1950s was a cultural role limited to men, and one for which she was not prepared). Other experiences of sensuality might have effectively portrayed more familiar aspects of feminine experience, like the sexual juiciness which accompanies women's sensuality. I choose to tell Aunt Tina's story because it is her autonomous image that enters the field of the work and calls for voice.

## AUNT TINA: SENSUAL GODDESS

Aunt Tina, my father's oldest sister, owned a bridal salon in Trenton, New Jersey. On my frequent visits there, summers exploded with play and exotic activities. Heady shopping trips for clothes, Bermuda shorts with matching tops, bikini bathing suits, and new shoes meant magic to me, a kid growing up in a coal-mining town where most fathers crawled into the blackness of the earth each day, where one new outfit for school filled all material desires. These shopping trips heralded the beginning of great adventures, and spending enormous amounts of my aunt's money on the wild extravagance of pleasure-seeking trips to amusement parks, ice cream shops, and the Atlantic City Boardwalk. At the center of these holiday outings, like a starburst, was Aunt Tina.

As a 9 year old, I was enraptured by her glorious ability to seize each day. The contrast between her and my beautiful mother set me on fire with wonder. My mother worked raising three, four, and then six children in Ashley, Pennsylvania. She prayed the rosary daily. Her goal was to bake, to mother us, and to help the nuns at Holy Family Church. She performed immeasurable acts of kindness for the old Polish ladies of our neighborhood. Mother was slight and gentle. Her idea of an outing, at least when I bothered to notice, was an evening at the Bingo games.

Aunt Tina had a grainy, booming voice. Her eyes were alive with mischief and adventure. She was short with a huge butt and a hairstyle that rivaled Betty Boop's. Never did she allow anything on her feet but spiked heels, which forced her to walk in such a manner as to make her outrageous butt stick out even more. Her love and commitment to her many nieces and nephews were as tidal waves through our lives.

She always held a lit cigarette between her fingers. Those fingers appalled and intrigued me, as each nail was painted a brilliant red. My mother often said, "Red nails are the work of the devil." Yet, I knew there was nothing of the devil in Aunt Tina. As evidence, my mother and she were bonded members of a mutual admiration society, bordered on all sides by a fierce love for my father, a wanton addiction to poker, an abiding exasperation toward my grandmother, and a love for us children. And as mothers and daughters sometimes share an unspoken language, my mother communicated to me that the devil comment somehow excluded Aunt Tina.

Those nails fascinated me, perhaps because Aunt Tina fought a losing battle with a nail biting compulsion that rendered her nails stubby. Ordinarily, one would not call attention to them with a glossy flash of red. But there was Aunt Tina, "out there," owning herself and her pleasures. When I looked at her, this voice inside called, "Yes!" I learned much later in life that parents can transmit a range of affect to their children, by simply experiencing them, embodying them. In such a way, her flood of natural exuberance carved its own river in my soul.

Aunt Tina is the only person I know up close who could simultaneously communicate uncompromising disapproval and unadulterated love. She, more than anyone else in my life, embodied the adage, "dislike the act, not the person." She scolded me if I committed a social gaff, allowed me to vacuum her bridal salon, and conveyed with clear certainty that to touch or, God forbid, soil one of her exquisite gowns would never be allowed or excused. There was never fear on my part, or hers, that that forbidden act would happen. Her trust in my competence and perfection was absolute. Her laughter and pleasure in life and in me diminished the power of all threats.

Watching her with her clients was sacramental. To my preadolescent eyes, her joy in each bride's beauty was real and vibrant. Her easy dancing between mother and daughter with wit and charm brought elegance to her and to them. What a striking contrast between her manner and the understatement of my mother. Today I visit teachers around the country presenting seminars. I find that my laughter and love for them flows freely. We bond; we dance around the challenges of their work. We solve problems and enrich each other. Aunt Tina brought this talent to me. If it is true that the seeds of talent are ours at birth, then she was its watering fountain. Watching her feast at the table of human interaction was my training ground.

One day at the Atlantic City Boardwalk, my sister JoAnn, cousin Eileen, Aunt Tina, and I went to the fun house, the kind with the mechanical fat lady out front, slapping her knee and endlessly laughing. Once inside, we carried on, scaring ourselves senseless with fake cries of terror. Passersby, hearing our screams, which grew riotously out of hand, chose not to partake of the fun house. We, of course, were oblivious to this. At each lost sale, the owner grew angrier.

As we four approached the exit, we found ourselves in a massive rotating barrel. With each attempted step forward, the barrel turned, pulling our feet to one side. Losing our balance produced waves of hysterics. Oddly, the owner grew angrier.

Aunt Tina croaked, "Oh my God," as she fell on top of me. Our laughter and craziness escalated; her weight on me was monstrous. Eileen, then JoAnn joined the heap; I remained buried, praying for the slow movement of the barrel to relieve the crushing weight.

Someone yelled, "God, I just wet my pants." It was Aunt Tina.

I felt the warm trickle on my back amid more laughter, then an astonished confession by JoAnn, "I peed my pants too." We no longer attempted to exit the barrel. In complete abandon, we rolled and laughed and screamed like four pickles in a pickle jar.

At that point, the owner stopped the ride. In the abrupt stillness, which seemed to disorient us all, spittle draining from the corners of his mouth, he began yelling, "Get out. Get out and don't come back."

As we drunkenly staggered from the exit, the looks on the faces of the gathered crowd communicated unequivocal disapproval and disgust. We were untouchables, basking in our own solidarity. The four musketeers, shameless, stinking at the crotch. We were full of life's greatest gift, joy. That's how I remember Aunt Tina, master of exuberance, re-creator of the word love. A love that manifested itself in a full-throttled blasting into our world.

By the time I was 23 and preparing for my wedding day, 13 years had passed between that exile from the fun house and 1970, the year of my wedding. My mother had died in 1962, which resulted in my experience countless testimonies to the worthlessness of motherless daughters. Aunt Tina was a whole state away when other mothers were cooing over the beauty or specialness of their female offspring. I was often sad, always alone during those years. And so with wedding preparations underway and very little money, I made my pilgrimage to Aunt Tina's bridal shop.

As I look back these 26 years later, I understand that my journey was that of a salmon swimming upstream; I was going home. Much as in the old days with those countless brides before me, she fussed and approved, bringing balm to my hungry soul. In her boundless presence I was transformed, suddenly the owner of a worth and beauty that was my heritage. Through her careful ministry, I appeared in the mirror in a breathtaking gown, whose celebration of Juliet sleeves and rich lace spoke of taste and grace.

And then there appeared a headpiece too astonishing even to have been hidden in my dreams. Handmade in Germany, its base was a four-inch wide band covered by a masterpiece of intricately adorned flowers and confection. It orchestrated my face as nothing has before or since, bringing out elegance in my jawline and a doe-like beauty to my eyes. That headpiece drew out everything exquisite that lay inside me. Aunt Tina pooh-poohed the cost of the gown, and to this day I have no memory of what I paid or didn't pay. I could only hear in her generosity to me a testimony of my worth as a young woman. Only other daughters who have faced adolescence and rites of passage without their mothers could understand the magnificence of her gift to me.

Kindness—how far it reaches into sorrow and abandonment. How it transforms us, as if by fairy dust, into beautiful spirits whose lives hold potential and wonder. I have not thanked her enough over the years, but I have made her legacy of life and love my own. Many friends have spoken of my kindness, my angel-like guardianship of their hearts' secrets and hopes. My students have told me that I make learning magical, that fun reigns supreme in my classroom. Like Aunt Tina, I boom at them, demand of them, but most of all, powerfully love them. I am dancing the dance she brought to my life many years ago. This generosity of mine is my tribute to Aunt Tina, the woman who taught me what absolute pleasure feels like, the woman whose kindness replaced the shame of being motherless with blinding evidence of worth.

I wonder now as I think of her, owner of her own business, married yet independently defining her own sense of vitality; why we women look too much to men to bring us flowers and affection when it is so often the women in our lives who have sustained us, enriched us, and nurtured us. Perhaps this is why I write this, my woman's story, a call to women to treasure each other.

## BELIEFS AND AFFECTS IN THE FIELD

My personal experience of being this woman's niece and sharing many moments of her life is that I remember laughter: hers and mine. I remember the brilliant twinkle in her eyes, a wonderful counterpoint to her deep booming voice that seemed scary but never deeply so; thus one had the sense of escaping an archetypal and tragic devouring event, a recurring escape which gave me a sense of heroism. I was a wily girl child eluding some imagined wrath of which she seemed capable. This sense of her dark aspect became more noticeable when we played poker, an activity in which I was allowed to join at the age of 9. She would growl, "In poker you have no friends." I knew at those times to be respectful of a darkness, which lurked close to consciousness. Paradoxically, I was simply and eternally safe because I was hers and she was mine.

With her I was never isolated, but always the recipient of women's secrets: her displeasure at this or that action of her mother, her exuberant devotion to and love of her brothers, her disregard for her husband's boisterous threats about matters that seemed significant to him and not to her, like when she was not ready for church on time. He was an usher, and that seemed to be linked to an attitude that he could never be late. He would threaten to leave her at home, and she would yell at him like a lioness. They seemed to be quite comfortable with the colorful arguments and threats that accompanied such tension. My own mother never yelled at my father; thus, I found Aunt Tina's response intriguing and admirable.

With Aunt Tina, I remember the joy of excess within a felt framework of containment, although that may seem a dichotomy. We ate outrageously large ice-cream sundaes, for which we received "Pig Badges," which we wore home with pride, spent money, then more money, and caroused late at the Atlantic City Boardwalk. Of the abundance of pleasure and fun, I have one overriding response in the present: I had so much of its counterpart in my life that the hedonistic perspective she brought to my early life was enriching and sustaining.

To say I loved her seems too poor. I embraced her. I inhaled her. This woman owned the cosmos and threw it to me, as one throws a colorful beach ball in a grand water game. Being in her realm brings to mind the words in *The Prince and the Pauper*, "The difference between a prince and a pauper is not who they are but how they are treated." I was royalty because I was hers. Because we continue this relationship imaginally, I continue to believe that I am entitled to life's celebrations.

I believed that if she could live as she did, then so could I. If she could fully love, fully rail, abundantly eat and prance, and wear red nail polish and spiked-heeled shoes, so could I. If she could have her own business, I could do anything I choose.

Her life was a statement that a woman's light shadow needn't be kept in darkness, that each woman need only exercise her birthright: to claim contained excess, dark emotionality, fierce capacities to love, rail, and prance—all those qualities of both light and dark power that squirt like fountains from the depths of feminine being. I grew to womanhood in a patriarchal culture in which the Dark Goddess's qualities of greed, sexuality, and hate were carefully and complexly kept away from human consciousness but in Aunt Tina's sphere, I experienced a good measure of those qualities transformed and contained by goddess energies made conscious through a lived life. I therefore have the experience of moments in which life is enriched because it is whole, of both masculine and feminine principles.

## *PROUD SEXUALITY AND INSTINCTUAL CONNECTION*

The Sensual Goddess is free. Hers is a realm of proud sexuality, instinctual connection, relatedness, and flashfloods of emotions. From my experience of her, her defining characteristic is her juiciness. When she seeks to know what is real, she goes within, finding what she seeks in feminine ontology. She's independent, and interdependent. She adorns herself; she loves her body, its scent, its transformative nature, and its blood mysteries. She brings her fullness to all domains of worldly expression, and her talent flowers because she takes responsibility for it. I am struck by the

stark difference and cultural unfamiliarity, even today, between this sensual woman archetype and the maternal feminine archetype that lives in
societal light; and I write this story about sensual energies that spilled into
the world through my aunt as an invitation that other expressions of the
goddess may more easily manifest in societal consciousness.

With the perspective of a child of the 1950s and a young woman of the
1960s and 1970s, comes a "third wave" of feminist women who are more
familiar with the light shadow aspects of talent, sensuality, sexuality, and
passionate creative initiatives of the goddess. This means that, for many of
them, the sensual impulse toward expression is closer to consciousness. To
learn more about current feminist critique and experience, read Heywood
and Drake (1997). Additionally, poignant personal accounts in Listen Up:
Voices from the Next Feminist Generation, present portraits of the "third
wave" of feminist experience, attesting to the lived reality of the emergence of the cultural feminine shadow (Findlen, Ed. 1995). This shadow
figure struggles nonetheless against a 5,000-year history of cultural repression (Whitmont, 2001).

I often experience a deep admiration for the many young women with
whom I come in contact, who do choose to embrace the responsibility
early on, for the realization of their talents, and their dreams. My own
daughter is one such young woman, working and living in New York City
and Brooklyn, fulfilling her vocation as a performing artist, bravely facing
rejection and public critique (even as she is acknowledged for her talents
and achievements). Yet, she keeps in consciousness the sensual experience
of being in her work, living out of her passion, knowing that the vitality of
her soul's expression rests, for now, in daring to embrace her artistic work.

My life now is one in which I venture forth to bring what is in my
mind and soul to the public forum. This study is one such example. As a
woman who has struggled with Ereshkigal (Meador, 1994) to reclaim her
feminine grounding, such claiming of talent was not always so. In the past,
I sought out others who I believed to be leaders, whose vision I admired,
throwing my energies into their causes, which too easily became my own.
As I was not conscious that I lived in the Suns of others, I did not realize
that I chose not to claim my own deeper talents, so that I would not have to
take the responsibility for my gifts; the light shadow is in shadow because
it is unconscious.

Yet, to engage in relational and family related activities seemed to be
an appropriate choice for me, and in retrospect continues to feel right, a

gift for which I shall always be grateful. Read Miller's (1986) seminal discussion of the psychological development of women, in which she writes that women grow in-relationship, do have particular feminine capacities, like the ability to consider how various life choices impact those with whom they relate, how personal power is not as defining as relating in terms of growth. The scholarship of Jordan, Kaplan, Miller, Stiver, and Surrey (1991) also inform the current discussion of the particular ways in which women develop, which until articulated by the feminist critique has been marginalized by masculine constructed theories of development.

As I parented, as I supported my husband professionally and personally, and as I spent 39 years as a teacher, satisfaction and expression imbued my life. Yet to fulfill my Sensual Goddess fate meant to venture out to the public forum with my writing, my scholarship, to make my deeper contribution, and to live in subtle and profound personal ways the Sensual Goddess archetype. This passionate creative activity of soul, this project toward my intimate and independent passion, didn't happen for many years for me, and perhaps needed my own maturing, my own healing and psycho-spiritual development, before it ripened into its present form.

For me, to envision and evaluate educational initiatives, to design effective mental-health programs, and to write all somehow seem to be alive in the present, requiring the consciousness of the Sensual Goddess.

## THE CONSTELLATED ARCHETYPAL FIELD

Just as it is difficult to find women heroines in myth, with the exception of the true myth, Joan of Arc (Brunel, 1992), it is difficult to find this Sensual Goddess in the cultural imagination, as western mythology is constructed within the patriarchal world view, where sensuality is often misunderstood and feared, thus kept below.

However, as I look to cultures that valued women in all their aspects, I discover that the image of the Sensual Goddess appears in early Mycenaean and Minoan civilizations, civilizations about which, Dexter (2001) writes, "The feminine played a central role and (at least in Minoan Crete) women held significant positions in society" (p. 153). In this early culture, the image of the Sensual Goddess is so compelling a symbol of fecundity and regeneration after death that her image as a woman with frog legs, and hands which expose her vulva, remains visible over centuries in Christian cathedrals in Europe (Dexter, 2001). The frog-shaped goddess appears in many civilizations; a common name is Heket (around 3100 B.C.). She is the primordial mother of existence. From Dexter (2001), we learn that "Heket has been connected with the Greek Baubo" (p. 28). In addition to displaying her vulva, she sometimes raises her skirt in an exuberant, invitational gesture that possibly dates to Neolithic skirt-raising rituals (Dexter, 2001). The Baubo archetype lives today in classic poses in pornographic depictions of women, a shadow expression which objectifies the feminine and too often provides a poor substitution for lived relationship. Her archetype finds positive expression also behind the closed doors of lovers who choose consciously to acknowledge her lusty possibility in sexual exchange.

## GODDESS MYSTERIES IN THE VIETNAM VETERANS MEMORIAL

In modern culture, the positive aspect of the Sensual Goddess is currently being articulated by literal women, who live out of the goddess's instinctual energies. Her impulse resides in the juicy creativity of modern women who have entered societal consciousness through public expression. An example of one such woman is Maya Ying Lin, who, as an 18-year-old Yale student, offered her design as one of 1,421 others for consideration for the Vietnam Veterans Memorial (Swerdlow, 1985). Her design, created for a class on funerary architecture, has become a healing fountain for a culture torn apart by war's betrayals.

A fearless connection with blood and the earth is the hallmark of Lin's design, a black granite chevron, which cuts deep into the ground, elegantly listing the names of each American who died in the war. As one might expect from a work grounded in the instinctual feminine, it was Lin's wish to honor the land and also not be afraid of destruction as a fundamental expression. She writes, "I wanted to work with the land and not dominate it. I had an impulse to cut open the earth...an initial violence that in time would heal" (Swerdlow, 1985, p. 557). Lin describes her intention as she began her work; one is clear that she is not removed, not lost in abstraction, not fixed, not afraid to change notions about healing and mourning, therefore, not attempting to work within the constrictions of the masculine principle. Her sensuality is in the embracing of the earth, the relational, in her not flinching as a sensual being in her approach this memorial.

Of the bravery one faces in holding her talents and creations to the light of public scrutiny, Lin writes, "The first time I saw the granite panels, the place was frighteningly close to what I thought it should be. It terrified me to have an idea that was solely mine be no longer a part of my mind, but totally public" (Swerdlow, 1985, p. 557).

Sensual, instinctual, feminine construction has as a central attribute, the ability to do what is foreign in ego consciousness: to graciously hold the tension between multiple realities (Tarnas, 1991). Thus, creative acts that emerge from such a consciousness are often culturally confusing and misunderstood, by the larger society. As an example, in response to Lin's design, on October 13, 1981, a Vietnam veteran appeared before the Commission of Fine Arts and called the design a "black gash of shame" (Swerdlow, 1985, p. 567). Many other voices joined him in the national dialogue, initially misunderstanding, experiencing the monument as unheroic, unpatriotic, below ground, and death oriented.

What finally quieted this unrest was the sacred and instinctual participation of the public, especially and including the veterans themselves. No one anticipated the profound need to touch the names, the healing reconnection with a nation's lost sons and daughters, or the introspective joining that came from the reflective quality of the granite panels, reflections which seemed to join the living with the dead. The monument itself has become a place of neither/nor experience of soul. It is neither fully a place of the material world, nor a place of mind. It signifies a dual reality of the darkness of the nation's wound, a gash in the country's soul, and also a monument literally and symbolically facing the light of the sun, bringing the war home to its rightful place in national identity.

Of the moist, generative quality of the monument, particularly in its 60,000 engraved names, Swerdlow (1985) writes, "The names have a power, a life all their own. Even on the coldest days, sunlight makes them warm to the touch. Young men put into the earth, rising out of the earth. You can feel their blood flowing again" (p. 573).

This imaginal reality is linked to the depths of the feminine body/soul and the masculine response to its mysteries; the inner realms of the sensual goddess are magic; that which is lifeless is resurrected by the possibilities of her depths.

The manner in which names would be listed had been a source of dispute between the veterans and Maya Lin. The vets wanted the names listed in alphabetical order to prevent exhausting, long searches for loved ones; theirs was a masculine, practical, efficient approach. Young Maya Lin disagreed, voicing her opinion that an alphabetical listing would make the memorial look like "a telephone book engraved in granite, destroying the sense of profound, unique loss each name carried" (Swerdlow, 1985, p. 571).

Today, as one approaches the granite chevron, a veteran sits before a large book, with names listed alphabetically. Upon request, he gives the number of the panel on which an individual name resides; the panel corresponds to a particular tour of duty, signifying the point in the conflict when each man and woman served, providing both a personal and an epic telling. Lin knew, with a feminine sensibility, the importance of the story to healing, and could imagine the ghosts speaking through each name and particular time of service. Because her vision was grounded in the emotional depth of the Sensual Goddess, she was able to make a conscious and public stand.

I remember going to the wall for the first time with my brother Jim, a Vietnam veteran. At the time, he lived in Colorado, I in California. When I approached the monument, I was struck with the disorienting initial perspective from above, that the memorial seemed not to be present. I realized that I was experiencing the odd reality of the monument having been situated in a cut deep in the earth, and was therefore, below me. It was as if I stood at a sheer cliff, the granite panels being the cliff itself, directly below my feet.

After walking down a path to the level at which the granite wall could be viewed, my brother and I walked to the veteran who held a book and the names. Jim asked for the location of three names and said to me, "I have three friends I want you to meet." For the first time since he returned from Vietnam, 28 years earlier, he spoke to me of his experience there, through the story of his close friends, telling me who they were as men, how they died, and the part he played in their final days.

Out of respect for his experience, I will not speak in detail of my brother's response to the monument, but only about my own. The invitation of the wall toward intimacy, sharing of grief, reflection, and relational joining was for me sensually healing, full of the dark, internal, moisture of the feminine, full too of her powerful and often frightening emotion, desperately needed in allowing a nation finally to feel its profound loss. Lin's design of the monument was a gift to a nation, first and foremost because it honored men and women who lived out patriotism in ultimate contribution, and also because it brought feminine, sensual expression to the public forum, when only that transformative aspect of psyche would suffice.

I invite others to recognize the emergence of the Sensual Goddess, support her personal and cultural birth, and recognize sensuality as that deep, juicy part of self that is the honey pot of feminine consciousness, what Goodchild (2001) describes as clitoral consciousness. It is the Sensual Goddess, upon whom the fate of the earth depends. Ego consciousness has been won at the price of cultural, feminine repression in both men and women (Tarnas, 1991), and will now stand or fall as the Goddess is embraced or denied. The decision to consciously choose her is perhaps the final imperative of the postmodern project.

****************

CHAPTER FOUR

# THE GARDEN REVISITED

This study of imagination began with a dream in which I encountered a beautiful though neglected garden, and witnessed an otherworldly Japanese dancer, a psychoidal figure, who profoundly moved me, and has stayed with me, guiding me from outside, just as other figures have, through the course of the work, provided assistance from within my psychic center. The following words partially describe my interpretation of the dream, and link the image of the garden to the exploration of imagination within these pages, especially in its intention to uncover knowledge and experience about the reality of the imaginal realm. The full interpretation of the dream is in the introduction section. I wrote:

> I knew that my own ghosts, who brought the dream and also lived within it, would guide the work, asking of me embodiment and a joining with them in expression. Experiencing them, with the exception of the dancer, to be representations of the manifest self (my own psychic center), I could trust their guidance.
>
> That the structural under-girding of the garden is still visible though somewhat muted conveys a sense of feminine relatedness in the imaginal. The garden also suggests birthing and groundedness in the earth. Such grounding and birthing relate to the central challenge of my project: to grow that which, until now, lay dormant, and in dusky neglect, intricately woven within a matrix of possibility. (Harrell, 2002, p. 8)

With careful attention to each story, I have sought to unlock the comings and goings of imaginal figures, not as theoretical concepts but as illuminations that flow from experience, asking of myself and my reader fluid and soulful inquiry. Seven stories from my woman's life, seven snapshots captured the reality of the imaginal realm: fully participating, fully real, and fully mediating the realms of matter and spirit.

Psyche—my divine center—is a steadfast partner and coauthor of the work. It is her participation that allows me, even urges me, to identify these seven stories as being particularly resonant, as holding a vibrant, dynamic, and sacred quality. Throughout these pages, it is psyche, along with the consciousness imaged by the psychoidal figure in my early garden dream, which sends soulful intuition, and dreams that guide me, or approve of choices made along the way.

It is psyche who points to hidden mysteries behind the symbols in my stories, she who insists on sacred containment in which the imaginal and I tumble about until richly veined character reveals itself, much like stones ground smooth and glistening in deep tidal dances. In her care, all the imaginal figures fully emerge to tell their stories of transformation: the joy of the lively grasses, Inanna's confusion in an unknowable and alienating underworld, redemption born on the broken wing of a red-tailed hawk, and others. Thus, psyche is for me a friend and creator and, at the same time, deeply linked with each image within the stories.

You likely know all too well that the work of uncovering hidden meaning in these pages is heuristic in nature, as I am both depicted and depicter in each story. As a depicter I take responsibility for structuring the experience to be explored, and more importantly, as meaning is discovered, I keep my gaze on myself, a being of body, spirit, and soul, the depicted. I tell the story and also maintain visibility, as a psychological being and as a transforming, becoming woman. My purpose is not to expose myself; by now you have seen me revealed as a flawed and vulnerable figure. I do this to sing a soul-song of love fulfilled, of imaginal and sensate beings connected across space and time, and always as a dance of fate fulfilled. My work is and always has been an invitation to others to join me in the wonders of enchantment.

The hermeneutics within each story is multilayered; it is a quest for deep understanding of the figures in this domain, whether they be intrapsychic, psychoidal, or cultural, whether they are personalities, archetypes of transformation, intuitive feelings, or impulses. Simultaneously, it is a search for the hidden mystery in the imaginal landscape, the search for the Hidden God.

Three streams of questions move throughout my stories, having been asked throughout this book, I repeat them here: (1) The imaginal realm: what do my memoirs tell about how the imaginal world works, how she manifests, how she becomes more or less real in my experience of her, what this realm illuminates, and how this illumination unfolds. What part do I—my soul, ego, persona, affects, beliefs—play in her illumination? (2) The figures within the *mundus imaginalis:* what does the investigation of these stories tell us about the figures that live within the domain of imagination, particularly their differing levels of reality, their nature, their source, and their response to engagement? How or why do these imaginal figures deepen interiority and bring forth transformation, for me and for my readers, as they choose to enter the realm of imagination? (3) Methodology for psychotherapists: what can psychotherapists take from this study to enrich them in their clinical practice?

The stories and reflections in the study itself are rich in imaginal analysis and should not be summarized here. Instead, I present highlights of the findings that respond to the questions raised. I underscore that although most scholars mentioned throughout the preceding chapters have expressed these ideas in theoretical terms, my investigation is unique in its focus on experience.

## THE NATURE OF THE IMAGINAL REALM REVEALED

There were identifiable moments of consciousness in my stories, when the imaginal world broke through. Breaking through means that the imaginal realm becomes more real. I experience this realm and become altered by her mediating function, become changed as my organ of imagination allows me to experience the sensible world and the world of mind, through an intellect of soul. Until I focused on the phenomenon of imagination as a series of lived experiences, I was not aware that the breakthrough of this realm is announced with an altered consciousness, an awareness. Yet, I discovered also that this consciousness is complex, as discussed below.

I described throughout the stories specific moments when the imaginal realm broke through. In those moments when the veil of the in-between world parted, a resonant and soulful gnosis entered consciousness. In the story I called "Raptor," I wrote:

> The hawk, so very large at this close distance, his chest held high, simply lifted his eyes and looked into mine with the clearest intention,

meeting my gaze like a king. His expression, like none other I had seen
before allowed both of us to flow into the soul of the other. (Harrell,
2002)

It is noteworthy that in that identifiable moment, although there was consciousness, there was a paradox of experience: both a knowing (a soulful
awareness) and also a muting, a tendency to miss the importance of the
moment, that this was a moment of breakthrough. One quality of the experience, which caused a lowering of conscious awareness (the muting of
soulful experience) in the example above, was fear that the large raptor
would harm me with its talons as I attempted to lift him off the road.

In acknowledging a gathering of Crone women in Chapter 3 which I
named "Stories from the Shadowlands," I noticed that some wise women in
the group had actually lived before me, and some who are much younger
would most probably reach cronehood later than I (in a present not yet
realized). Yet I was moved that in the imaginal realm where I experienced
them, they seemed in a space-time dimension that included what I can
best describe as a past, present, and future, experienced in only present
time, and in what I will call same-space, the space where crone women
and crones-to-be could be imagined as being together as actualized crones.
There are two paradoxical realities in this example—one, the reality of
women in one space and time, the present, and also a societal, more
ego-related reality, in which some of these women are dead, some living,
and some too young to be crones.

Additionally, my experience of time in the imaginal realm suggests
that it does not possess the urgency that it does in the modern sense.
For instance, several years have passed since events in the "The Raptor"
occurred, and 52 years since my first visitation by my figure in "Unbidden
Angel," yet I had not identified, in the fuller, deeper sense, the moments of
breakthrough, nor did I fully, consciously understand the meaning of those
breakthrough moments until I did the contemplative work within these
pages. The time that has passed between experience and enlightenment
was long, by societal standards, but seemed irrelevant in the timescape of
the unfolding soul.

Because the imaginal realm is inhabited by autonomous figures from
the unconscious (and in the case of psychoidal figures, from a realm outside), there is a need to respect that they also possess agency and purpose,
and therefore one must not try to control or to push for certain outcomes,

but must trust that the purpose of the experience will unfold in its own way and in its own time. For example, I have been haunted for decades by the psychoidal figure in the story titled "Unbidden Angel," haunted especially by needing to know what she had in the box; what was so important a gift that she came again and again, trying to deliver its contents to me over those many years of visitation. It was during the alchemical work of this study when the angel and I met in the transformative field, that I was able to experience her without fear, and was able to allow my soul to know her intention, that I finally understood what she carried in the box and wrote about that in my study:

Had I been able to allow a relationship with my figure she would have brought me knowledge about my life, similar to that which my personal mother would have given me in my adolescent years and, because of her nature, knowledge beyond the personal. The box "of flowers" was a gift of illumination. (Harrell, 2002, p. 82)

I learned as I reflected on the seven stories in this study that just as the mind and body remembers, so does the soul. Thus, the hermeneutic quest for meaning must sometimes wait until the soul is ready for transformation, and perhaps at times, *needs* to wait until the self and the ego develop a stronger relationship.

I claim that the *mundus imaginalis* and its numinous figures can be experienced within a broadening societal consciousness, the consciousness of many of us, as opposed to esoteric initiates. If others, non-esoterics, wish to visit the enriching realm of imagination, then a contemplative stance is needed, much as in the practice of dream work, where one keeps a journal, writes the dream, then later when the complex that accompanies the dream is no longer constellated one begins to consider the images, the affects, and to look for associations; this is the search for the Hidden.

The examination of personal affects and beliefs was critical to each chapter, and is important for others to consider because these are often held in the unconscious, yet they decidedly define and color the contents of the figures that manifest, giving them shape and particularity, but not creating them or causing them to exist.

What I have discovered in this work is that any person, like the esoteric, must pay a price to enter the *mundus imaginalis*, that is, she must adopt a stance of looking, gazing, or focusing on that which wants to be known.

What I had understood only conceptually, until I fully experienced it in the process of entering this in-between world was the imaginal realm's dual, interconnected quality of ambiguity and depth. This appreciation of ambiguity and depth was opened to me in the transferential field within this work. By transferential field I mean the dynamic space in which my topic worked me over, changed me, and informed me, even as I encountered my topic. In this field, I experienced differing depths of hidden meaning beneath the symbolic. For instance, behind the symbol of the hawk in the story titled "The Raptor," I discovered the archetype of descent, and later, as the hermeneutics continued, I discovered that behind the material hawk, the outer symbol, was the Hidden God (Corbin, 1998).

The ambiguous attribute of the depth most surprised me in that I experienced it as extending both down into the realm of the unconscious but also up into the heavens, as in the moment when I simultaneously reached down to lift the raptor (and, more surprisingly, my wounded soul) and by that same act reached up to a Divine, who simultaneously reached down to me in a moment of mutual sympathy and compassion. More surprising still was the discovery that further depth, and yet another layer of ambiguity, transformed into meaning, as I realized that the Hidden God was the angel within, my very center.

Consciously to experience these recursive, multidimensional attributes of the imaginal realm for me was like playing at the ocean where the sand meets the tide day after day, feeling full and alive, then one day, going out to a coral reef in a diving suite and oxygen tank, and diving below the surface, to swim for the first time beside magnificent fish, and colorful, coral formations. The former experience is joyful and enriching; the latter adds a new dimension of being, an ecstasy.

As this project began, I wondered if engagement with the imaginal realm causes her to manifest. After participating in and gazing upon this world during this study, I believe that the imaginal field is always present, always manifest. It was I whose eyes were closed to the soulscapes that were present. It seems that, though I discern the imaginal, I am a being, like most others, whose material body and capacities of mind are profoundly limited and confined in terms of how much I can observe, organize, process, and psychologically and emotionally contain. Although I can hold the tension of differing realities, I can do so only within the limits of my human organs of perception. But the imaginal realm does not bow to these human constrictions. Thus, I do not bring forth that complex imaginal world, which is present whether or not I gaze upon her.

The imaginal can appear to manifest, much as the sun appears in the sky, in a more real way, when we notice it, feel its warmth, and enjoy the quality of filtered light it brings to a forest floor. What allows me to see what is already present is focused engagement: looking at and interacting with. As I reflected on the cultural dream in the story titled "A Nation Dreams Its Violence," in which gruesome images of destruction and the repressed chthonic feminine appeared to manifest, I described the way in which my experience of the imaginal changed as I focused on her:

> I observe that engagement with the imaginal causes it to become more fully illuminated, more real, more colorful, more replete with image, and more enlivened. It is as if the imaginal is always present but requires conscious intention to host her, in order to achieve visibility, meaning—as in the example of my experience within this memoir— that one must choose to contemplate the events as imaginal reality as well as phenomena of mind and matter. In the act of providing hospitality, the dream's images became boldfaced as the "bold" font on a computer causes certain selected words to become more visible, more valued in the discourse. So, too, does the engagement of and attention to, the imaginal cause me to see beyond the veil of an in-between world, even though such seeing is limited by the degree to which I am able to tolerate the disorientating onslaught of negative affect and somatic disturbance that accompany even intermittent consciousness of the real. (Harrell, 2002, pp. 153–154)

Thus, I wish to clarify that in the experiences told within these pages, in both the telling of my stories as well as their meaning-making reflections, I did not, could not, cause the imaginal to manifest, nor did I cause personal or archetypal figures to appear. Rather I attended, responded, and created the soulful stance wherein I saw that which matter and mind, when experienced without the mediating intellect of imagination, keep hidden.

In addition to attending, responding, and creating a soulful stance, I played another role in the illumination of the symbolic. I became aware, as I entered the alchemical field of the study itself, of the necessity of an observing mind and an open heart. As I contemplated the moments of breakdown, in the reflections that followed the stories I named "The

Raptor" and "I Am Inanna," I was focused on finding meaning, consciously working within the imaginal realm while simultaneously being aware that my observing mind was active in the project.

This need for an observing consciousness is not something I take for granted because encounters with the imaginal occur within a framework of soul, and at times, in the experiences within the imaginal stories, I was in a state closer to an undifferentiated ego consciousness than one usually experiences. In the imaginal realm one functions, in good measure, out of the feminine principle, especially in the ability and necessity to hold the tension of multiple realities. Therefore, as I searched for meaning I was required both to allow a dimming of consciousness and also to maintain a reasonable mind.

I have previously written that there is also an important distinction between causing the imaginal realm to manifest and having one's beliefs and affects color the particular attributes of the manifestations within the field. To illustrate, I recall the story titled "Crones in the Shadowlands," in which the imaginal realm manifested in a dream. The imaginal field, within the dream and in my waking state before I slept, smelled of betrayal, orphanhood, neediness, and blowing smoke in an effort to obscure a shadow activity of soul, betrayal.

My belief system and my affects shaded the images that manifested in the mundus imaginalis. I believed, rightly or wrongly, that the old ladies who inhabited the small coal mining town where I lived my early years, lived without healthy, interactive, and vibrant masculine relationships. And so, when psyche wished to call upon the image of crone consciousness, to nudge me to a better path, my beliefs about and memories of these women who surrounded me as a child gave particular detail and color to the archetypal image of the crone. This quality of imaginal figures being shaped by the feeling-toned experiences and beliefs of the imaginer does nothing to curb authenticity. Rather such personal feelings and beliefs help us with associations and meaning making. That is why I devoted so much time to them as I explored the imaginal and why your analyst will always ask for your associations when exploring a personal dream.

My beliefs and affects relative to masculine relatedness at that time in my life when the old women appeared, penciled in the character of the husband figure in the crone dream. Although I associated negative attributes to this dream figure husband and related those attributes to my unconscious experience of my personal, estranged husband, I do not equate my associations with literal facts. Yet, psyche does not care about that which is discernable fact, but rather about that which the unconscious perceives as relevant. Therein lies her value to transformation. She sees what the senses and the mind do not.

## BEINGS WITHIN AND WITHOUT

I discovered much about the figures in the imaginal realm, which I experienced as unique, ambiguous, changeable, and fluid representations of self. More importantly, I experience these figures as autonomous independent beings in the mundus imaginalis, beings within my psyche and without.

There is the figure of the Japanese dancer, a real figure who is not a part of my psyche but who was sent by the Self as a subtle body, a friend, possessed more of Divine essence than any part of my psycho-spiritual self. Additionally, the figure in the story titled "Unbidden Angel" was clearly outside my psyche; she also is Other. The dancer and the angel are not I, nor are they representations of my center of being. These psychoidal figures are evidence of Hillman's (1983b) idea of soul's purposefulness, or soul's telete. Those figures are sent by the Self to bring me into relationship with the Divine (Raff, 2000).

How do I determine that the dancer and the angel are real figures that exist outside? The unconscious, the imaginal, is essentially a feminine, intuitive realm. One's feelings must lead the way in finding meaning and understanding. Hegemony has marginalized intuition as other than a valued intellectual capacity. With the quiet emergence of the cultural feminine and a valuing of her capacities, there is a revaluing of intuition and feeling as sources of knowing. The tradition of depth psychology has contributed a vast body of literature that values the unconscious. The unconscious is understood as an expression of the feminine principle, as opposed to ego consciousness that is understood as related to the realm of the masculine.

One navigates through the unconscious domain by intellectual capacities that are both of the ego aspect of self, and of the unconscious-the rational, and the intuitive spectrums of knowing. I remember presenting dream interpretations to my psychodynamic therapist—a man for whom psyche is real, as are the figures she sends to the imaginal realm—only to have him ask, "And how did you feel as this dream action was occurring?" If the feeling did not support the interpretation, the interpretation was questioned, reexamined. Image, affect and instinct must be in harmony for the resonant response to be present, felt by the imaginer, the dreamer, the soulsinger. It is this resonance for Johnson (1986) and me that is a test of illumination.

Therefore, one's resonant feeling affirms whether or not the psychoidal figure is outside, beyond one's psycho-spiritual beingness. Using my intuitive intellect, I described the Japanese dancer in my initial dream with the following words: "What is most striking is that the numinous quality of the girl's movements—her grace, her blending of music, form, body, soul and spirit—are not of this world" (Harrell, 1999, p. 6).

I knew also that the figure in the story titled "Unbidden Angel" was not a part of my psychology. That discernment, however, seemed more obvious because she existed in a subtle state, not fully material and not fully spirit. She was a non-corporeal being; her thoughts spoke to me, her heart spoke to mine, and she possessed a power and agency that was undeniable. She was experienced to be "more real" than the Japanese dancer. What is interesting to me is that I clearly and consciously experienced this psychoidal nature of the figure, over 50 years ago, before I understood the concept of the imaginal realm, and long before I heard the term psychoidal figure. My soul knew. It is depth psychology, particularly analytical psychology, that has given language and a scholarly conceptual frame in which to articulate her very real nature.

Archetypal figures entered my stories, adding the experience for me of yet another quality of realness; their individual effect on us seems profoundly mitigated by the psycho-spiritual state we bring to the imaginal encounter.

In the story I called "I Am Inanna," two archetypal figures presented themselves to me, Inanna, and Ereshkigal (Meador, 1994; Wolkstein and Kramer, 1983) and because of a personal individuality I brought to the encounter, I was able to experience one figure as more real than the other. In the paragraphs to follow, I shall try to explain this phenomenon—experiencing one figure as more real than another—as it occurred in my study.

As a mythopoeic figure, Inanna represents the archetype of going down to a lower realm, a place below cultural consciousness, below the realm in which the masculine is dominant. Inanna is the imaginal figure that represents the quest of every woman who seeks her feminine grounding, her feminine consciousness, that part of self in men and women that the culture denies or mutes (Meador, 1994). In my story, I clearly shared

Inanna's affective experience of the underworld, and this sharing of affect, even identifying with it, rendered Inanna more real to me.

On the other hand, Ereshkigal represents darker, more feared aspects of the feminine. Ereshkigal is linked to a woman's wish to live in her Sun, her own identity. Ereshkigal is the erotic impulse. Her archetypal character contains or devours that which the society chooses not to see, such as greed and aggression (Whitmont, 2001). Ereshkigal is the symbol of the powerful, emotional, and expressive potential of the feminine.

I could identify with Inanna's emotional suffering. As she endured and experienced the underworld, so could I. Her archetypal image in my dreams and in the re-telling of the memoir allowed me enough connection, and at the same time, enough distance, to be in the archetypal moment, the moment of descent, imaginally and fully emotionally.

In experiencing Ereshkigal, I could understand her, know her, and clearly feel her rage. I learned from her. I find that my transformation has resulted in much more introspection, more self-reflection and caring for my personal interests as I am invited to join the passions or vocations of others. Taking care that my interests are represented is not a quality that the broader culture supports in a woman. Because of her consciousness, I am much clearer about what and whom I serve when I choose to give my energy and commitment to a project or initiative.

Yet there exists a caveat to my experience of Ereshkigal. Although I am able to understand her rage at Inanna, I am not able to identify with her emotion, to experience rage at my situation. Just as the archetypes are the broad forms of human experience, individual effects of the archetypes on each of us are differentiated, experienced individually, and uniquely.

I could not really feel my own rage at what happened to me: finding myself alone in a central California farming town, with very few friends, a daughter, and extended family on the other side of the country, and in serious financial difficulty. I could not fully feel the rage, for instance, when I attempted to open an account at one of America's older merchandise chains, and was denied credit because I "had no credit history." I, who had worked for 25 years of my life and in my marriage, paid my bills on time and often early. It was my husband, and not I, who somehow got "the credit" for my part of our family's financial responsibility. No one denied him credit when our marriage ended. "Why did our stable and responsible financial history benefit him and not me?" I asked, even though I knew the answer: the patriarchy overvalues males, their contribution, their leadership, their presence in family business.

I could not feel rage because it seemed so immense that it would crush me, suffocate me; it could open floodgates to other affronts, other cultural attitudes in which the masculine was overvalued. One such affront came when, toward the end of our marriage, my husband took an education position 400 miles from our daughter's high school. I chose to stay in the family home for 1 year, with her, so she could finish high school. I would join him afterward, and she would not have to attend a fourth high school because of his changing professional situations.

My superior at work took me aside (as did several other friends) and made sure I understood that if I did not go with my husband, did not support him by moving also, that I would "not be welcomed anywhere, in any home, or at any public (meaning social) event." This was not his view, he said, but how others felt. One friend said it differently, "You need to go with your man." I could not believe this response. It was 1995, and I was a feminist woman and an educational leader, with an impeccable reputation. This affront threatened to overwhelm me, had I allowed myself to feel the rage that it brought to me.

I learned through experience that although the archetypal figures we meet in the mundus imaginalis bring us forward, their appearance in our lives is not a magic cure. They cannot make us feel the affects, which they represent, but only invite us to do so. They are representatives of human experiences, not a means to avoid or transcend experience. Thus, I may meet the archetype imaged by Ereshkigal again, when I am better prepared to identify with the rage she represents. And at such time, in my experience of her, she will be more real.

## WHAT CAN THERAPISTS DO?

Implications of this study of the imaginal realm for psychotherapists are as follows: Early in the writing, I wondered how knowing the imaginal realm and her figures might inform the practice of psychotherapists. Although my intention was to increase knowledge of the imaginal realm by entering its field as a researcher and participant, insights have been gained which I believe can allow therapists to be more helpful to patients. In this section, I will try to be specific and to hold the stance that some of my readers may not be familiar with imagination as a therapeutic tool, and will write so that a broad group of readers will understand. I will not exhaust all the possibilities within the stories, but wish to give some examples of practice.

From the story titled "The Raptor," we learned that healing can be found in images that take us beyond societal experience. Therefore, when a patient comes to a session with a story about a seemingly insignificant encounter (i.e., finding an animal on the road), what may be hidden behind the outer experience is the transforming Divine. The work of the therapist is to create the alchemical space for the illumination to unfold. This may be achieved by the therapist asking, "Can you describe the beast, its gestures, its expression, as if its presence is with us in this room?" By this intervention, the imaginal is invited to enter the session. This process also describes Spiegelman's (Spiegelman and Mansfield, 1996) interactive field, where the unconscious constellates, and image becomes a participant in the field.

To be aware, as therapist, of a patient's subtle body states, as well as what images manifest, can deepen the work also. To help guide a patient toward physis/psyche mutuality is part of the healing process. For instance, I wrote in this study about a dream in which an exquisite rising sun caused me to wake with a deep physical sensation of calm and well-being. The symbol of wholeness in the dream was accompanied by a corresponding physical state, linking psyche with matter.

The literature on finding meaning behind archetypal figures advises that one goes to the fairy tales and myths (Von Franz, 1996) when personal associations are limited. The dream titled "Bringing Up the Dead," in Chapter 3, and its interpretation and my subsequent action in the outer world, is a good and practical example of how one actually puts the fairy tales, the image, and the affect together, and then follows this work with changed behavior.

I was recently invited to address a group of therapists at State University of New York, Oswego, on dream work. As I had been asked to focus on an analytical psychological perspective, I shared the dream titled, "Bringing Up the Dead." The class members reported that this part of the presentation was especially helpful because the notion of archetypes and their relationship to dream work had been a mystery to them, although they were somewhat familiar theoretically with imaginal psychology.

The portrayal throughout the study of the dynamic relationship between the image and the complex is useful to practicing therapists. For example, in the story titled "I Am Inanna," there was the moment when a friend asked, "Why do you continue to love a rejecting and absent husband?" Out of that question came the image of the teenage child who sat slumped and alone, clearly identified by me (the imaginer) as the figure of abandonment. That moment of naming and recognition was the beginning of curing, or at least shifting the abandonment complex, or more broadly stated, the negative mother complex. Aizenstat (1996, unpublished lecture) says that to cure, one must first name the god who visits. In my story, the god, or archetype, is that of abandonment. Second, he says, "One must honor the god" (Aizenstat, 1996, unpublished lecture). By this he means that one must host the image and relate to it in its reality in the therapeutic moment. My story gives one example of this hosting, as my friend, a therapist, supported and guided me in this work. Image is linked to experience and affect. Thereby to host, the image brings forth the experience of the complex and the affect that belongs to it. The tears I cried as I hosted the abandoned teenage girl were healing, bringing me, body and soul, into the experience of abandonment. It was the complex itself that had blinded me to what really held me to this unhealthy relationship. Until I was able to be soulfully and consciously present with the image, soul life leaked out of my being.

Perhaps the most significant therapeutic understanding that the study unveiled for me is the following paradox. To approach the imaginal realm is to be in a highly differentiated state of consciousness that can also require a simultaneous move toward an undifferentiated ego state. This paradox, in which differentiation and undifferentiation of ego states exist simultaneously, seems to be an acceptable and necessary condition for discovering that which is hidden behind the outer image. Such a dichotomy is discussed in depth in Chapter 2, in the story of the red-tailed hawk (the raptor). For my ego state to be "lowered," as in an early stage in the evolution of consciousness (Neumann, 1954/1995), so that I could merge with the hawk, allowed a transformation that, in terms of soulwork, was extraordinary. As a therapist, I am in a better position to guide my patients in their search for the hidden, deeper reality behind the image, because of my own understanding, and meaning-making experience in "The Raptor" story, and the reflection that followed.

## HOW DOES THE EXPLORATION OF IMAGINATION FOSTER DEEP GROWTH?

This study opens several avenues for further exploration. I believe it would be informative to design a study in which readers who are unfamiliar with depth psychology would share their perceptions of the world before and after reading the stories and reflections in this study. The question would be, in what way does reading stories about life that is experienced through an imaginal lens change the reader's experience of his or her life?

To clarify, I belong to a writers' group composed of university professors. My group members are published scholars from several disciplines: linguistics, education, social science, and women's studies. For them, depth psychology is not a familiar field, yet they have read most of the stories in this study and have asked probing and insightful questions. They have reported to me that the work has changed the way they see the world. To focus on this changed perception might be fruitful in the development of imaginal epistemology.

As an associate professor in a School of Education, I was involved in partnership initiatives with public education in which public school teachers, preservice teacher candidates, and university professors teamed together to improve learning in the schools. A project with a middle school teacher and a classroom of at-risk seventh-grade students is one which was found to be illuminating. The goal of the project was the tending of soul and also exploring adolescent literature themes, impulse control, and introspection.

The students and teachers (the classroom teacher and myself) explored crime, which was presented in the literature, and wondered what internal voices might impel one to crime or lead one away from crime. The adolescent learners created artwork in which their imagined inner voices became compelling visual images. In doing so, they worked with archetypal processes and also developed a deeper capacity to look within their experiences. The work also invited a relationship with the unconscious.

The art and interview material—in which the students, in deeply moving personal voice, shared their human experience—informed both the students and the many other educators who later saw a presentation of the art. Further work of this nature, which was clearly an expression of the constellated unconscious field, would allow exploration of the way in which adolescent youngsters experience the imaginal realm.

## REVISITING THE GARDEN

In the discussion above, I offer analysis and an intellectual view, in highlights, of the study's findings. The imaginal nature of this book calls for an ending that is imaginal. Therefore, I wish at this point to revisit a dream, which came at the beginning of this study and to interact, through active imagination, with the garden, which I first experienced as an image in a dream. I begin with a re-telling of the dream as it appears early in this work:

> I get out of a car and approach a home in the country. On the porch to greet me are many members of my family. I notice as I climb the path toward them, that an old garden encircles the home; years of neglect and overgrowth do not obscure the great design and beauty that claims it still. Its paths, weaving here and there, and its variegated shades of greens and multi-textured shrubberies, speak of a marvelous structure that undergirds the garden. What I witness, speaks too, of a gifted and loving gardener.
>
> As the group (curiously lacking in animation) observes my approach, I see what they do not, that to my left and their right, dances a young girl, dressed in Japanese classical garments. What is most striking is that the numinous quality of the girl's movements— her grace, her blending of music, form, body, soul and spirit—are not of this world. In the dream, I struggle to find some way to organize the otherworldly experience. I am frustrated because I try to experience it with my senses and knowledge of the world and find those capacities inadequate. My frustration is nothing though, in light of the wonder and beauty of her dance. (Dream Journal, 1999, p. 53)

## THE DANCER AND HER DANCE

The most compelling image in this dream is the beauty of the dance. The consciousness of the dancer and her dance has been with me throughout this study. Even now as I write, as has often happened, I can see her. She is still dancing; she is still in the garden, still otherworldly. When I imagine her, she commands my gaze, rendering everything else in the space as so much background music. Doing the writing and reflecting in the study has been many things for me: sacred, illuminating, difficult, demanding, frustrating, and disorienting. But her presence in the work has been a con- stant invitation and inspiration. At times I lost sight of her, but it was I who failed to look, or could not be contemplative, and even then I knew with the organ of imagination that she was there. Her dance symbolizes that soulwork is Divine hermeneutics, an encounter with the Hidden God. I know that she is not an aspect of my interiority, as clearly as I know that when a church bell sounds outside my home, that my ears did not make the sound, but rather simply perceived it.

## DIFFERING QUALITIES OF CONSCIOUSNESS

The group on the porch, curiously lacking in animation, has become more than a broad representation of a societal consciousness that does not see the Japanese dancer or the potential beauty and mystery of the garden, the imaginal, feminine realm. Each member of that ragtag lot represents specific aspects of societal consciousness that also entered the work through my personal identification with their unfruitful, unimaginal attitude.

At times, consciousness was a wish to serve ego, rather than the work, or a dead feeling of sluggishness, or a lumbering sense of personal stupidity, or being overwhelmed in my attempt to manage the tension that this complex work brought forth. Sometimes individuals within this group represented the many demands of my role as a university professor. Over the course of writing this book, there were meetings, a teacher preparation program to help write, papers to grade, classes to teach, and other research projects that demanded attention. These were all the aspects of ego consciousness that grounded my being but also demanded a much different focus on my time and my consciousness, a looking away. When I experienced life through these other, very real, aspects of consciousness, the work of tending the garden moved more slowly.

## THIS BECOMING GARDEN

Nonetheless, it has been the garden that has been foremost in the imaginal space, in the past several years. The garden and the imaginal field are the same. Each story in which meaning was sought, in which neither/nor possibilities were considered, each dream interpretation, each numinous revelation—these were all the work of tending the garden, birthing, and regenerating the imaginal realm.

In daily experience, I tend to think of gardening in a romantic way, not focusing on the sweat, on the boulder that refuses to budge and needs more than the gardener for movement to occur. I am not concerned about the drought or the heavy rains that are sure to come, or conscious of how my joints and muscles will ache from being in an odd position for too long. I tend instead to see myself in fantasy, in a flowing sundress and a large straw bonnet, tenderly placing roses in an open basket, or at the very least, imagining the warmth of the sun and the vibrant blooms that will come, in gratitude to me for the tending.

The real work in nurturing the imaginal, in making a contribution to a reclamation of an imaginal way of knowing, has called upon the many faces of the gardener's experience—the pleasing, the frustrating, and the backbreaking. But the work has been difficult, not at all romantic. When I found boulders too heavy to move, my advisor and mentor would work with me, her own initial work in the imaginal field helping me move the boulder, breaking it apart with a suggestion, a framework, a question. Simply asking, "How does this passage deepen your theme, or how does this link to the purpose of the study?" would pulverize a boulder that blocked the work. I alone could not move it because I could not see it. My outside reader would call my attention to a particular section of the work, or a particular perspective and say, "That took courage to write," or "That passage will help all of us who study this field." In those moments it was as if a fellow gardener noticed an especially vivid bloom and called, "Come see this. It is wonderful. Put down your shovel and come to celebrate."

The garden now, in my active imagination, does look different. One can see patches of blooms that have been fertilized and watered, blooms that receive just the right quality and intensity of sun. There is not an abundance of these clumps of color and life, but that they are present at all is enough. They are the promise that what is required is the presence of the loving gardener, of other soulsingers. Each clump of color is an illumination that the study brought forth.

Even as I look I can clearly see the dancer, moving in and around these groups of blooms, energized by them as I am by her presence. And the paths have become "traveled paths." The garden looks like a place where someone works, where people who appreciate her beauty come and notice and tend. This is a becoming garden, far from finished; it is a becoming place because this study has tended some aspects of the imaginal realm by rendering them visible.

In my imagination, I see a gathering of figures, witnesses to the work. They approve and are deeply connected to this garden. They have a stake in its renewal. I experience these figures as I did the gathering of the crones in Chapter 3, "Stories from the Shadowlands." I know them. They are Mogenson's (1992) angels, those who are no longer alive in a material way; blood which once flowed through their veins is now replaced by ichor that flows through the veins of the gods. They live in the *mundus imaginalis*, and are the figure of a hawk with the attitude and gaze of a king, a Madonna, the non-corporeal being who floats as if in a Mexican procession; they are old crones with white hair and a straw pipe, Aunt Tina, with her Betty Boop hair and her spiked heels. I even see two boy shooters, without the archetype of violence owning and driving them, thankful that someone spoke of a truth that is bigger than they. I see the Sensual Goddess, and even my friend, Kara, the Mexican red wolf. There is Inanna and Ereshkigal. All of these dwell in the garden as figures in a medieval painting, without the treatment of modern perspective that renders them objects. They are as real as the flowers, the boulders, and I.

# REFERENCES

Abrams, M. H. (1999). *A glossary of literary terms* (7th ed.). Orlando, FL: Harcourt Brace College Publishers.

Ansbacher, H., and Ansbacher, R. (1964). *The individual psychology of Alfred Adler.* New York: Harper Torchbook.

Aizenstat, S. (1996, October 26). Unpublished lecture, Pacifica Graduate Institute. Carpinteria, CA.

Bachelard, G. (1971). *The poetics of reverie: Childhood, language, and the cosmos* (R. Russell, Trans.) Boston: Beacon Press. (Original work published 1960)

Barnhart, R. K. (1995). *The Barnhart concise dictionary of etymology* (1st ed.) New York: Harper Continuum.

Becker, U. (Ed.) (1994). *The continuum encyclopedia of symbols.* (L. W. Germer, Trans.). New York Continuum. (Original work published 1992)

Beyerbach, B. & Davis, R. D. (Eds.). (2011). *Activist art in social justice pedagogy: Engaging students in glocal issues through the arts.* New York: Peter Lang, Publishing, Inc.

Brunel, P. (1992). *Companion to literary myths, heroes and archetypes.* New York: Routledge.

Capra, F. (1991). *The tao of physics: An exploration of the parallels between modern physics and eastern mysticism.* Boston: Shambala.

Cloud, J. (1999, October, 12). Just a routine school shooting. Time, pp. 34-36.

Corbett, L. (1996). *The religious function of the psyche.* New York: Routledge.

Corbin, H. (1989). *Spiritual body and celestial earth: From mazdean Iran to shi'ite Iran* (N. Pearson, Trans.). Princeton, NJ: Princeton University Press. (Original work published 1960)

Corbin, H. (1997). *Alone with the alone: Creative imagination in the Sufism of Ibn 'Arabi*. Princeton, New Jersey: Princeton University Press.

Corbin, H. (1998). *The voyage and the messenger: Iran and philosophy*. (J. Rowe, Trans.). Berkeley, CA: North Atlantic Books. (Original work published 1990)

"CROCODILE SCARS," YouTube video posted by National Geographic, June 27, 2008, https://www.youtube.com/watch?v=wc9dGK8ketg.

Culbert-Koehn, J. (1998, March 28). Unpublished lecture, Pacifica Graduate Institute, Carpinteria, CA.

Dexter, M. R. (Ed.). (2001). *Marija Gimbutas: The living goddesses*. Berkeley: University Press.

Girard, F. (Director) (1998). *Red violin [Motion picture]*. France: Red Violin Productions Limited, Sidecar Film.

Goodchild, V. (2001). *Eros and chaos: The sacred mysteries and dark shadows of love*. York Beach, ME: Nicolas-Hays.

Grahn, J. (1987). *The Queen of Swords*. Massachusetts: Beacon Press.

*Grimm's fairy tales, the complete*. (1972). New York: Pantheon Books, Inc.

Guggenbuhl-Craig, A. (1977). *Marriage-dead or alive*. Zurich: Spring Publications.

Guggenbuhl-Craig, A. (1979). The archetype of the invalid and the limits of healing. Spring, 29-41.

Harrell, M. H. (1986). *[Personal Journal]*. Unpublished data.

Harrell, M. H. (1998). *[Dream Journal]*. Unpublished raw data.

Harrell, M. H. (1998). *[Personal Journal]*. Unpublished raw data.

Harrell, M. H. (1999). *[Dream Journal]*. Unpublished raw data.

Harrell, M. H. (2000). *[Dream Journal]*. Unpublished raw data.

Harell, M. H. (2002). *[Personal Journal]*. Unpublished raw data.

Harrell, M. H. (2003). *Journey to imagination: A woman's lessons about life and love*. Unpublished dissertation, Pacifica Graduate Institute, Carpinteria, CA.

Harrell, M. H. (2010). *[Personal Journal]*. Unpublished data.

Heywood, L. & Drake, J. (Eds.). (1997). *Third wave agenda: Being feminist doing feminism*. London: University of Minnesota Press.

Hillman, J. (1983 a/1975). *Archetypal psychology: A brief account*. Woodstock, CT: Spring Publications.

Hillman, J. (1983 b). *Healing fiction*. Woodstock, CT: Spring Publications, Inc.

Jaffe, H. L. C. (1983). *Pablo Picasso*. New York: Harry N. Abrams, Inc.

Johnson, R. A. (1986). *Inner work: Using dreams and active imagination for personal growth*. San Francisco: Harper Collins Prublisher.

Jordan, V., Kaplan, A., Miller, J. B., Silver, I., & Surrey, J. (1991). *Women's growth in connection:Writings from the stone center*. New York: The Guilford Press.

Jung, C. G. (1954/1985). The practice of psychotherapy: Essays on the psychology of the transference and other subjects. In R. F. C. Hull (Trans.), *The collected works of C. G. Jung* (Vol. 16). New York: Pantheon Books.

Jung, C. G. (1960, 1984). The structure and dynamics of the psyche: Including "Synchronicity: An acausal connecting principle. In R. F. C. Hull (Trans.), *The collected works of C. G. Jung* (Vol. 8). New York: Pantheon Books, Inc.

Jung, C. G. (1953/1977). Two essays of analytical psychology. In R. F. C. Hull (Trans.), *The collected works of C. G. Jung* (Vol. 7). Princeton, NJ: Princeton University Press. (Original work published 1953)

Jung, C. G. (1961/1989). *Memories, dreams, reflections* (2nd ed). (A. Jaffe, Ed.; R. and C. Winston, Trans.). New York: Vintage Books. (Original work published 1961)

Jung, C. G. (1959, 1990). The archetypes and the collective unconscious. In R. F. C. Hull (Trans.), *The collected works of C. G. Jung* (Vol. 9. I). Princeton, NJ: Princeton University Press. (Original work published 1959)

Jung, C. G. (1991). Answer to Job. In R. F. C. Hull (Trans.), *The collected works of C. G. Jung* (Vol. 11). Princeton, NJ: Princeton University Press. (Original work published in 1958)

Kharitidi, O. (1996). *Entering the circle: Ancient secrets of Siberian wisdom: Discovered by a Russian psychiatrist*. New York: Harper Collins.

Lin, M. (2000). "MAKING THE MEMORIAL," The New York Review of Books (November 2, 2002): 1-7. Accessed September 4, 2014. http://www.nybooks.com/articles/archives/2000/nov/02/making-the-memorial/?page=2.

"MAYA LIN: WHAT IS MISSING," YouTube video, an interview with Maya Lin, posted April 26, 2012, https://www.youtube.com/watch?v=0cF-bLBQ9J-A&feature=em-share_video_user.

Meador, B. (1994). *Uncursing the dark: Treasures from the underworld*. Wilmette, Illinois: Chiron Publications.

Miller, J. B. (1986). *Toward a new psychology of women*. Boston: Beacon Press.

Mogenson, G. (1992). *Greeting the angels: An imaginal view of the mourning process*. Amityville, NY: Baywood Publishing Company, Inc.

Moustakas, C. (1990). *Heuristic research: Design, methodology, and applications*. Newbury Park: Sage Publications.

Neumann, E. (1971). *Amor and psyche: The psychic development of the feminine*. (R. Mannheim, Trans.). Princeton: Princeton University Press. (Original work published 1956)

Neumann, E. (1955, 1983). *The Great mother: An analysis of the archetype*. (R. Manheim, Trans.). Princeton: Princeton University Press. (Original work published 1955)

Raff, J. (2000). *Jung and the alchemical imagination*. Main: Nicolas-Hayes.

Raff, J. (2001, June 3). Unpublished lecture. Denver Athletic Club, Denver, CO

Rilke, R. M. (1978). *Duino elegies*. New York: W. W. Norton and Company.

Romanyshyn, R. D. (1992). *Technology as symptom and dream*. New York: Routledge

Samuels, A., Shorter, B. & Plaut, F. (Ed.) (1996). *A critical dictionary of Jungian analysis*. NY: Routledge.

Sardello, R. J. (1999). *Freeing the soul from fear*. New York: Penguin Putnam Inc.

Shinoda Bolen, J. (1991). *Wise-woman archetype: Menopause as initiation* [audiotape]. Boulder, CO: Sounds True Recordings. (Recorded at the "Knowing Women" Conference in Del Mar, CA).

Solomon, Andrew. (2014, March). The Reckoning: The Sandy Hook killer's father tells his story. The New Yorker, pp. 36-45.

Spiegelman, J. M., & Mansfield, V. (1996, April). Physics and the psychology of the transference. *Journal of Analytical Psychology*, 41 (2), 179-202.

*Standard dictionary of the English language: International edition*, vol. 1. (1964). New York: Funk and Wagnalls Company.

Swerdlow, J. L. (1985, May) To heal a nation. *National Geographic*, 167(5), 555-575.

Tarnas, R. (1991). *The passion of the western mind: Understanding the ideas that have shaped our world view*. New York: Ballantine Books.

von Franz, M. (1996). *The interpretation of fairy tales*. (rev. ed.). Boston: Shambhala.

Walker, G. W. (1985). *The crone: Woman of age, wisdom, and power*. San Francisco: Harper San Francisco.

Wikipedia, s.v. "List of school shootings in the United States," accessed September 3, 2014, http://en.wikipedia.org/wiki/List_of_school_shootings_in_the_United_States.

Wikipedia, s.v. "Pearl High School shooting," accessed March 14, 2014, http://en.wikipedia.org/wiki/Pearl_High_School_shooting.

Whitmont, E. C. (2001). *Return of the goddess*. New York: Continuum.

Wolkstein, D. & Kramer, S. (1983). *Inanna: Queen of heaven and earth: Her stories hymns from Sumer*. New York: Harper and Row.

Woodman M. (1985). *The pregnant virgin: A process of psychological transformation*. Toronto: Inner City Books.

Woodman, M. (1990). *Dreams language of the soul* [audiotape]. Boulder: Sounds True Recordings.

# INDEX

~~~✦~~~

## A

Abandoned women 61
Active imagination 8, 49, 62, 134,
  136
Act of writing 7
Adam's frightening pattern of
  escalating 81
Affects and beliefs 2, 11, 72, 123
Afterthoughts 88
Analytical psychology 8, 82, 128
A Nation Dreams Its Violence 71,
  72, 85, 125
Ancient rite of manhood 78
Anima 4, 45, 46, 56
Archetypal character 90, 129
Archetypal constellation 28
Archetypal experiences 24
  death 24
  orphan 24
  the Great Mother 24
Archetypal Feminine 44
Archetypal field 104, 105
Archetypal figures 125, 128, 130,
  131
Archetypal impulse 91, 94
Archetypal mother 15, 16
Archetypal personifications 80
Archetypal qualities 75
Archetypal violence 79
Archetype of descent 31, 66, 124
Archetype of transformation 32, 48

Asperger's syndrome 81
Audience extraordinaire 13

## B

Baubo 114
Beauty of the dance 134
Beliefs and affects 11, 126
  in the field 41, 90, 102, 103, 131
Belief system 43, 126
Betrayal 48, 98, 99, 103, 126
Birth control 24
Birthing 5, 86, 102, 119, 135
Black gash of shame 115
Blessed Virgin Mary 23
Bodily gestures 4
  in dance 4
Body patterns 78
Box of flowers 26, 123
Breaking through experience 26
Bringing up the dead 131

## C

Catholic hierarchy 23
Central dream figure 75
Coffee Hour 8, 11, 12, 14, 15, 42
Coming home 15
Communion 23, 24, 25
Coniunctio 63
Conscious feminine 84
Consciousness 2, 4, 5, 7, 11, 14, 16,
  20, 24, 25, 39, 41 – 45, 47, 48,

# T

# U

# W

# Y

# Z

CPSIA information can be obtained
at www.ICGtesting.com
Printed in the USA
BVOW03s1950130117

473205BV00001B/47/P